Christian
Commitment
For the 1980s

Must We Choose Sides?

by
The Inter-Religious Task Force for Social Analysis

A Study/Action Guide

Editorial Working Group

ROSE ANCONA
Methodist Federation for Social Action
New York, NY

JOHN BOONSTRA, N. Amer. Reg. Sec.,
World Student Christian Federation
Co-Editor, *Radical Religion*
Berkeley, CA

PEGGY CASE
Episcopal Church Publishing Co.
Pontiac, MI

SHEILA COLLINS
United Methodist Board of
Global Ministries
TIA Women's Project
New York, NY

ROBERT L. DeWITT, Episcopal Bishop
Editor, *THE WITNESS*
Pres., Church and Society Network
Ambler, PA

MARGARET FERRY
Church and Society Network
Bear Creek, PA

JOSEPH L. HARDEGREE, JR.
Co-Editor, *Radical Religion*
Palo Alto, CA

DAVID KALKE, Worker-pastor,
Lutheran Church in America
Theology In the Americas
N.Y. CIRCUS
New York, NY

KATHLEEN SCHULTZ, IHM
Nat. Exec. Sec., Christians
for Socialism
Detroit, MI

GEORGE McCLAIN, Minister
United Methodist Church
Exec. Sec., Methodist Federation for
Social Action
New York, NY

HARRY STRHARSKY
Investigative Resource Center
Oakland, CA

MARY LOU SUHOR
Managing Editor, *THE WITNESS*
Ambler, PA

SANDY WYLLIE
Carpet, Linoleum Installer
Co-Editor, *Radical Religion*
Oakland, CA

Editorial Coordinating Committee

EDITOR
Harry Strharsky

PRODUCTION MANAGER
Peggy Case

PRODUCTION ASSISTANT
Brian McNaught

Peggy Case

Sheila Collins

Robert L. DeWitt

Kathleen Schultz

Harry Strharsky

Mary Lou Suhor

Special Thanks to:

Kay Atwater	Don Eunson	Loretta Strharsky
Joe Barndt	Richard Gillett	George Todd
Bill Berkowitz	Fred Goff	Hugh White
E.C.P.C. Bd. of Directors	Jean Rooney	Xanadu Graphics, Inc.
	Harlan Stelmach	

This publication was made possible by a grant from the Episcopal Church Publishing Company.

The cover design and art for the six title pages are by Rini Templeton, Picheta and the Data Center graphics collection. The remaining graphics in this volume are from Community Press Features, Boston, MA.

Contents

Orientation and Overview

Where Does This Guide Come From?

Christian Commitment for the 1980s is published by the Inter-religious Task Force for Social Analysis. A short note describing who we are and the process we went through to produce this book may be helpful to our readers.

In 1976 a previous study/action guide on the social mission of the churches was published by the Church and Society Network in collaboration with THE WITNESS magazine. *Struggling With the System/Probing Alternatives* made its appearance at the General Convention of the Episcopal Church of that year. The first printing was sold out in several months; a second printing is virtually exhausted.

The Episcopal Church Publishing Company, which funded the initial project, was faced with the question of whether to authorize a third printing, finance a revision or terminate the project. It commissioned a careful evaluation of the original study guide, seeking critical response from every known person or group who had used it. The survey produced three major recommendations: First, a continuing and growing need was identified for such a resource to serve a broader-based Christian constituency. This suggested that to drop the project would be irresponsible. Second, some of the material in the first edition was found to be too limited or dated. A thorough revision was therefore in order. Third, a more representative study/action guide could be produced if an inter-religious editorial group was formed to take responsibility for the new project's direction. On this basis, the task was begun.

The Episcopal Church Publishing Company

allocated funds to hold an editorial conference to initiate the new project. Invitations to join in the formation of an Editorial Working Group were extended to representatives of other progressive church networks and interfaith groupings who had already demonstrated a strong interest in collaborating on such a project during the evaluation process of the first edition.

Our editorial group includes representatives of the Methodist Federation for Social Action, the World Student Christian Federation, THE WITNESS magazine, the Church and Society Network, the New York CIRCUS, (an urban ministry of the Lutheran Church in America), the Board of Global Ministries of the United Methodist Church, *Radical Religion* quarterly, Theology In the Americas, Christians For Socialism and the Data Center project of the Investigative Resource Center. We are six women and seven men — people who are lay, ordained, or members of religious orders. Our religious affiliations are Roman Catholic, Lutheran, Methodist, Episcopal, Reformed Church of America and Disciples of Christ. With the exception of two members who have significant coordinating responsibilities for the project and have received part-time salaries, we have either given time from our jobs, our personal lives, or both, without pay.

Early on, we met to overcome a major weakness of the first edition — that it attempted to speak to too wide a spectrum of interest, to people whose experiences were too divergent. We decided to produce two volumes instead of one. The first would speak to people actively questioning the promise of the present order and beginning to pursue a systemic social analysis. The second volume would address itself to those who have done some theoretical work to understand the source of our social discontent, but were asking what we could do about it. This volume is the first of the two. Both underscore the reality that, as Christians committed to the gospel mandate of justice, we all need to deepen our understanding of the world about us and develop a clearer social analysis.

We organized several plenary meetings to determine editorial policy, to agree on a profile of the constituency for whom our work was intended, to define tasks and divide labor and to decide the substantive content of the volume. Then, working in smaller groups in different geographical areas, we completed specific assignments which were reviewed by the entire group. This was not the quickest, nor the easiest way to accomplish this task. We hope it may have been the most effective. Our readers must judge.

Serious discussion and debate of various theological and political points of view punctuated each successive editorial meeting. Many opinions were changed; some were not. Throughout this process, however, we have all held the firm conviction that there is no more serious and important task than to commit ourselves to and engage others in the struggle for a more just society.

In addition to adopting a collective editorial model for production of this book, we also encourage group process in its use. Following each set of selected readings, we constructed a group exercise meant to reflect the life experiences of our Christian constituencies. This should enable reader/participants to move from session to session conscious of the dynamics of the group process. In working to develop a clearer social analysis, study groups should provide an environment in which each participant feels comfortable enough to express his/her deepest personal convictions. New perspectives are arrived at by re-examining and setting aside old ideas.

The subtitle of this volume is "Must We Choose Sides?" This question is addressed implicitly throughout these pages and leads us to the further question: "Which Side Are We On?" That is not only the subtitle of our second volume but also the central issue of our commitment.

Why Is It Needed?

As a general rule, our bosses, schools, churches and the mass media — those opinion-makers who interpret daily events — teach us to see the world from the perspective of those who control the decision-making in our major institutions. Our history courses, for example, have emphasized the politics of bishops and kings, generals, presidents and industrialists. Our knowledge of church tradition has focused on the "great men" or "fathers" of the churches. The language used to interpret the economic and political changes which are occuring in the United States and around the world is the language of the propertied class which controls our government and our financial institutions.

This perspective never reveals the daily struggle of housewives, factory, farm and office workers — all of us who produce the social wealth and are now losing ground in the battle to create a better life for ourselves and succeeding generations. Members of the propertied class never expose the toll their decision-making has on us, the working people. Their world view and analysis doesn't consider how lay people, especially women, have made the church a viable community institution.

We believe that a new analysis of the world is not only necessary to our physical survival but is essential to our spiritual survival as well.

The perspective we explore in the following sessions is taking shape and being forged out of the daily struggle against alienating work and unemployment, racism and sexism, poverty and exploitation, political domination and cultural imperialism —injustices of all kinds.

The voices of the prophets manage to break through, albeit in surprising ways. As a modern ballad puts it, "the words of the prophets are written on the subway walls and tenement halls."

Those subways and tenements are often the settings for an endless series of horror stories which roll forth nightly on the late TV news: Murders, rapes, fires, rent strikes, unemployment, lack of heating oil, energy crises, etc. With so many seemingly unconnected problems coming at us — and just before bedtime — it is difficult to analyze and make connections; to see how we can make waves, can effect change.

A primary goal of this study guide is to give shape to an investigation of the realities of our national life; to help us toward an analysis of how problems are interconnected and why one class exploits another. By participating in the group exercises after each session, we hope to find clues, together, on how to impact the system with hope and conviction, rather than fall prey to despair and fatalism.

The overall title — *Christian Commitment for the 1980s* — carves out the constituency for whom the book was produced. Obviously, Christians are not the only committed citizens. But Christians have a biblical mandate to feed the hungry, clothe the naked, visit the prisoner, free the oppressed.

Christ's continuous denunciation of wealth and power and His promise that the meek shall inherit the earth provide a powerful stance that shakes at the very foundations of civil and religious power. Which brings us to sober reflection in these sessions around the question: "Must We Choose Sides?"

We can understand neither our own world nor what is required of us as Christians, however, if we are exposed only to the analysis of controlling class interests. We need to see the world as *our* world and how we as working people effect and are affected by what happens. Our view of the world is disturbing and conflictual. It also gives us

courage, deep vision and forms of human community which we are in desperate need of discovering. We, the editors, invite you to participate in our quest for social analysis as a study in personal and social strength and renewed Christian commitment.

What's In It?
Session 1: Ordinary People, Extraordinary Dreams

Perhaps many of us will feel that the dreams expressed by the "ordinary" people quoted in this session are not unlike our own, and therefore not "extraordinary" at all. What makes them extraordinary is that they cannot be fulfilled under working conditions enforced by the present economic order. This session and the following are aimed at investigating the question: "What kind of a society is it in which only a small percentage of the people have any chance of getting work which is fulfilling?" and "Can we do anything to change it?"

We are invited in the first group exercise to share our own experiences as working people (what we like about our jobs, what we find alienating and oppressing) and to share our own dreams.

Session 2: We Make History . . . Or It Makes Us

Having shared our personal view of life at work, we move on in this session to look at our experiences in historical context and to examine the workplace itself as part of a system. We investigate how work is organized, our participation (if any) in its control, the fundamental differences between workers and owners. The readings introduce a few concepts to help us begin to develop a social analysis. We also probe the question: "How is our religious practice influenced by our class background?"

Session 3: Confronting Capitalism

This session moves us deeper into systemic analysis, asking us to examine the structure of the capitalist system. First, a group of writers affiliated with a Christian missionary order take on the task of testing the myths of capitalism. In addition, a Canadian philosopher presents elements of a classic Marxist critique of capitalism. As the second reading points out, Marx did not think capitalism would fail because it is unfair or unjust, but because the system itself creates problems it cannot solve. Runaway inflation, massive unemployment and the continuing energy crisis are just a few indications that capitalism is creating sufficient problems to stimulate a radical critique of itself.

In this session we probe the reality behind words charged with political and moral responsibility — like "exploiter and exploited," "oppressor and oppressed" — which make us angry. We try to channel that anger constructively in a group exercise designed to explore not only the injustices of capitalism, but also the organized forces confronting those injustices.

Session 4: The Elements of Class

How do we understand class and where do we locate ourselves in the social strata? That is the burden of investigation for this session. So frequently we hear fearful reference made to the "class struggle," as though the very mention of it is to advocate violent upheaval. This session seeks not to advocate it but simply to recognize class struggle as a fact. The first reading examines what role people play in this production process, in decision-making, in control over what they do for a living. It contrasts what the tiny propertied class owns and controls to what the rest of us have.

The second two readings attempt to locate the churches in class struggle. Which class interests do the churches uphold? More often than not, the churches defend the interests of the propertied class. But because our churches are multi-class organizations, this is not always true. The prophetic Church has always taken up the struggle of the poor and working people. Our churches provide no sanctuary from class conflict in secular life.

The exercise for this session is a role play. It is designed to help us look at some of the hard questions we face in taking responsibility for the stewardship of church property.

Session 5: Reclaiming Our Christian Tradition

Why "reclaiming" in the title for this session? Because ever since the days of the early Church, the reigning political and social powers have fought to prevent the Christian faith from threatening their established way of doing things. Jesus was a champion of the oppressed, and God continues to "put down the mighty from their thrones and exalt the humble." But today, many know that religion is more preoccupied with its "spiritual" role and preserving the *status quo* than with exercising its prophetic role or becoming involved in social mission.

Yet, there have always been those who believe that there can be no real peace and love without justice, and that faith must be linked to practice, each informing the other. This session tries to help us to recapture that ancient tradition of the Christian faith.

Session 6: A Reform Is A Reform . . . Or Is It?

Finally we address the overwhelming question: "How do we organize to assure that we are not simply undertaking bandaid approaches to solve problems which have deep roots in the heart of our economic order?"

While there is no easy answer to this question, we are convinced that we have been involved in sufficient action and reflection since the 60s and throughout the 70s to summarize our experience of the past and develop a clearer direction for struggles continuing into the 80s. This session presents a few guidelines and a framework for group process so we can judge for ourselves whether our own current efforts will produce substantive reforms or not.

Some of us insist that we think our way into new ways of acting. Others argue that we act our way into new ways of thinking. It is our hope that this study/action guide will enable us to do some of both. It has been designed to help committed Christians like ourselves to break away from worn-out concepts and do some creative new thinking. Equally important, it should effectively move us to answer affirmatively the question: "Must We Choose Sides?", whereby we strengthen our commitment to the class-conscious struggle, and act our way into a new way of thinking.

How To Form a Group

Conceivably there is some value in reading this work by yourself, but it is intended to advance the churches' social mission where (at least) two or three are gathered together. Hopefully, this study/action guide will be an occasion for people to gather in small groups.

We all know many people who are disaffected with and confused about the world. Disaffection makes them feel that something should be done. Confusion makes them feel that nothing can be done.

Can you think of several such people within your parish and/or community whom you could interest in coming together for a series of meetings to pursue the development of a social analysis? This is all that is needed.

Size of Group: Up to 10 or 12 people make for a well-functioning study group. Experience indicates that 12 is not an arbitrary number. If there are more, the less articulate are excluded from discussion.

Commitment: There must be a commitment to spend a few hours reading and reflecting in preparation for each meeting and to follow through to the completion of the series of six sessions. However, your group may want to spend more time on one session than on another. If so, schedule an additional meeting. The *Appendix* at the back of this book should be a helpful resource and should be referred to throughout the course of your study.

Frequency: Again, general experience indicates that bi-weekly meetings are best. More frequent meetings are difficult to arrange and there is value in the personal reflection and reaction that takes place between meetings. Less frequent meetings tend to interrupt continuity.

Meeting Place: Anyone's home is a fine setting or rotate from one home to another.

Length of Meeting: A prompt time for meeting and for adjourning after not more than two hours is ideal.

Leadership: It is important to have someone designated as discussion leader for each session. If you wish to rotate this responsibility, fine. But if someone seems to be a "natural," take advantage of this. This does not exclude the possibility of rotating the responsibility for initiating discussion.

Group Process: It is important that there be a balanced interaction within each meeting session. Joint study and discussion, as well as group support for individual member's workplace problems, family, church and social concerns; and the celebration of common hopes are all important elements within a well-organized session. It is also important to have a brief evaluation at the end: "Was this a good meeting?" "Why?" "Why not?"

Sensitivity: This subject matter can be high-voltage. It touches some of people's most cherished and long-held attitudes and opinions. It is important for all in the group to be sensitive to the feelings and reactions of others. The discussion leader should especially be alert to draw people out — "How do you feel about that?" "Why do you feel so strongly about it?" Give people space for expressing emotion as well as reason.

Action/Reflection: If no action follows or accompanies study, then the study itself may not have been of much value. If some action does result, but is not evaluated in the terms of what we have been discussing, then it may well be a lesson unlearned. Reflection should lead to action and action requires reflection and evaluation. ∎

Ordinary People, Extraordinary Dreams

It is somewhat astonishing that, in a society in which the majority of people spend most of their waking hours either at work or worrying about the lack of a job, there are so few opportunities for people to come together to explore their workplace experiences or their roles as *workers*.

For most people, the world of work is a place of crucifixion. Listen to Studs Terkel's description of it in the introduction to his best selling book, *Working*, which consists of interviews with people from all walks of life who talk to him about their work experience:

"This book, being about work, is, by its very nature, about violence — to the spirit as well as to the body. It is about ulcers as well as accidents, about nervous breakdowns as well as kicking the dog around. It is, above all (or beneath all), about daily humiliations. To survive the day is triumph enough for the walking wounded among the great many of us.

"The scars, psychic as well as physical, brought home to the supper table and the TV set, may have touched, malignantly, the soul of our society. More or less. ("More or less," that most ambiguous of phrases, pervades many of the conversations that comprise this book, reflecting, perhaps, an ambiguity of attitude toward The Job. Something more than Orwellian acceptance, something less than Luddite sabotage. Often the two impulses are fused in the same person.)

"It is about a search, too, for daily meaning as well as daily bread, for recognition as well as cash, for astonishment rather than torpor; in short, for a sort of life rather than a Monday through Friday sort of dying. Perhaps immortality, too, is part of the quest. To be remembered was the wish, spoken and unspoken, of the heroes and heroines of this book.

"There are, of course, the happy few who find a savor in their daily job: The Indiana stonemason, who looks upon his work and sees that it is good; the Chicago piano tuner, who seeks and finds the sound that delights; the bookbinder, who saves a piece of history; the Brooklyn firefighter, who saves a piece of life. . . . But don't these satisfactions, like Jude's hunger for knowledge, tell us more about the person than about the task? Perhaps. Nonetheless, there is a common attri-

bute here: A meaning to their work well over and beyond the reward of the paycheck.

"For the many, there is a hardly-concealed discontent. The blue-collar blues is no more bitterly sung than the white-collar moan. 'I'm a machine,' says the spot-welder. 'I'm caged,' says the bank teller, and echoes the hotel clerk. 'I'm a mule,' says the steelworker. 'A monkey can do what I do,' says the receptionist. 'I'm less than a farm implement,' says the migrant worker. 'I'm an object,' says the high-fashion model. Blue collar and white call upon the identical phrase: 'I'm a robot.' *'There is nothing to talk about,'* the young accountant despairingly enunciates."

*   *   *

If our world of work is a place of physical and spiritual violence, as Terkel contends, then the inability or lack of opportunity to see *ourselves* as workers and to share that experience with others is one of the ways we have become alienated from our own suffering. If we cannot tap into our own sense of oppression in this crucial arena of our lives, then we may be unable to understand the suffering of others or even imagine that there might be a collective way to alter institutions and alienating social relations.

In this session we will be reading and discussing the work experiences of seven people as a way of preparing ourselves to look at our own experience as workers. The first four stories are excerpted from Studs Terkel's *Working*. We have chosen them because they represent a cross-section of the American labor force: Mike Lefevre represents the highly unionized heavy industrial sector; Larry Ross, the world of private sector management; Maggie Holmes, the non-unionized sector of the labor market heavily populated by women and Third World people; and Betsy Delacy, the burgeoning service industries, usually associated with the public sector. Min Chong Suk's story, which follows these four, was excerpted from a longer piece published by the American Friends Service Committee. We have included here only the most insightful passages. We believe it is important to look at what is happening to workers in the Third World because the conditions under which they work are directly tied to the economic and political structures of the dominant Western nations. In turn, the structure of our own workforce is increasingly shaped by what happens abroad. In exploring the conditions of working life, then, we are forced to think internationally.

If people are alienated and bruised at work, it is equally true that, in a society in which a wage confers dignity as well as the ability to survive, people are destroyed by unemployment. Rosie Washington and Alfred Prato reflect the other side of the coin of work in America. Their stories are excerpted from an article which appeared in the *New York Times Magazine.*   ∎

There are six readings suggested for this session (Rosie Washington and Alfred Prato's stories constitute one reading). They are all short and each can be read easily in five or 10 minutes. Count your group off by sixes; each person takes the reading which corresponds to the number they have taken. If you are studying with a large group of people, divide up into smaller groups of six each.

For each group of six people choose a facilitator to keep time and keep the process moving. The first five to 10 minutes will be spent reading the selections chosen. As you read, make a mental comparison between the life and work situation of the person about whom you are reading and your own lifestyle and work experience.

Working People Speak Out

Mike Lefevre
—STEELWORKER

I'm a dying breed. A laborer. Strictly muscle work — pick it up, put it down, pick it up, put it down. We handle between 40 and 50 thousand pounds of steel a day. (Laughs) I know this is hard to believe — from 400 pounds to three- and four-pound pieces. It's dying.

You can't take pride any more. You remember when a guy could point to a house he built, how many logs he stacked. He built it and he was proud of it. I don't really think I could be proud if a contractor built a home for me. I would be tempted to get in there and kick the carpenter in the ass (laughs), and take the saw away from him. 'Cause I would have to be part of it, you know.

It's hard to take pride in a bridge you're never gonna cross, in a door you're never gonna open. You're mass-producing things and you never see the end result of it. (Muses) I worked for a trucker one time. And I got this tiny satisfaction when I loaded a truck. At least I could see the truck depart loaded. In a steel mill, forget it. You don't see where nothing goes.

I got chewed out by my foreman once. He said, "Mike, you're a good worker but you have a bad attitude." My attitude is that I don't get excited about my job. I do my work but I don't say whoopee-doo. The day I get excited about my job is the day I go to a head shrinker. How are you gonna get excited about pullin' steel? How are you gonna get excited when you're tired and want to sit down?

It's not just the work. Somebody built the pyramids. Somebody's going to build something. Pyramids. Empire State Building — these things just don't happen. There's hard work behind it. I would like to see a building, say, the Empire State. I would like to see on one side of it a foot-wide strip from top to bottom with the name of every bricklayer, the name of every electrician, with all the names. So when a guy walked by, he could take his son and say, "See, that's me over there on the 45th floor. I put the steel beam in." Picasso can point to a painting. What can I point to? A writer can point to a book. Everybody should have something to point to.

. . . Hell, if you whip a damn mule he might kick you. Stay out of my way, that's all. Working is bad enough, don't bug me. I would rather work my ass off for eight hours a day with nobody watching me than five minutes with a guy watching me. Who you gonna sock? You can't sock General Motors; you can't sock anybody in Washington; you can't sock a system.

A mule, an old mule, that's the way I feel. Oh yeah. See. (Shows black and blue marks on arms and legs, burns.) You know what I heard from more than one guy at work? "If my kid wants to work in a factory, I am going to kick the hell out of him." I want my kid to be an effete snob. Yeah, mm-hmm. (Laughs.) I want him to be able to quote Walt Whitman, to be proud of it.

. . . Automation? Depends how it's applied. It frightens me if it puts me out on the street. It doesn't frighten me if it shortens my work week. You read that little thing: What are you going to do when this computer replaces you? Blow up computers. (Laughs) Really. Blow up computers. I'll be god-damned if a computer is gonna eat before I do! I want milk for my kids and beer for me. Machines can either liberate man or enslave 'im, because they're pretty neutral. It's man who has the bias to put the thing one place or another.

If I had a 20-hour workweek, I'd get to know my kids better, my wife better. Some kid invited me to go on a college campus. On a Saturday. It was summertime. Hell, if I had a choice of taking my wife and kids to a picnic or going to a college campus, it's gonna be the picnic. But if I worked a 20-hour week, I could go do both. Don't you think with that extra 20 hours people could really expand? Who's to say? There are some people in factories just by force of circumstance. I'm just like the colored people. Potential Einsteins don't have to be white. They could be in cotton fields, they could be in factories.

. . . Somebody has to do this work. If my kid ever goes to college, I just want him to have a little respect, to realize that his dad is one of those somebodies. This is why even on — (muses) yeah, I guess, sure — on the black thing . . . (Sighs heavily.) I can't really hate the colored fella that's working with me all day. The black intellectual I got no respect for. The white intellectual I got no use for. I got no use for the black militant who's gonna scream three hundred years of slavery to me while I'm busting my ass. You know what I mean? (Laughs.) I have one answer for that guy: go see Rockefeller. See Harriman. Don't bother me. We're in the same cotton field. So just don't bug me. (Laughs.)

After work I usually stop off at a tavern. Cold beer. Cold beer right away. When I was single, I used to go into hillbilly bars, get in a lot of brawls. Just to explode. I got a thing on my arm here (indicates scar). I got slapped with a bicycle chain. Oh, wow! (Softly) Mmm. I'm getting older. (Laughs) I don't explode as much. You might say I'm broken in. (Quickly) No, I'll never be broken in. (Sighs.) When you get a little older, you exchange the words. When you're younger, you exchange the blows.

. . . When I come home, know what I do for the first 20 minutes? Fake it. I put on a smile. I got a kid three years old. Sometimes she says, "Daddy, where've you been?" I say, "Work." I could have told her I'd been in Disneyland. What's work to a three-year-old kid? If I feel bad, I can't take it out on the kids. Kids are born innocent of everything but birth. You can't take it out on your wife either. This is why you go to a tavern. You want to release it there rather than do it at home. What does an actor do when he's got a bad movie? I got a bad movie every day.

Larry Ross
—CONSULTANT

The corporation is a jungle. It's exciting. You're thrown in on your own and you're constantly battling to survive. When you learn to survive, the game is to become the conqueror, the leader.

I've been called a business consultant. Some say I'm a business psychiatrist. You can describe me as an advisor to top management in a corporation. I've been at it since 1968.

. . . The executive is a lonely animal in the jungle

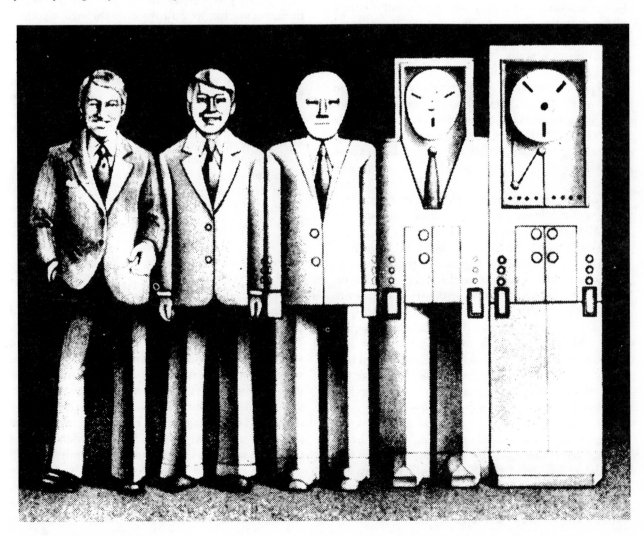

who doesn't have a friend. Business is related to life. I think in our everyday living we're lonely. I have only a wife to talk to, but beyond that . . . When I talked business to her, I don't know whether she understood me. But that was unimportant. What's important is that I was able to talk out loud and hear myself — which is the function I serve as a consultant.

The executive who calls me usually knows the answer to his problem. He just has to have somebody to talk to and hear his decision out loud. If it sounds good when he speaks it out loud, then it's pretty good. As he's talking, he may suddenly realize his errors and he corrects them out loud. That's a great benefit wives provide for executives. She's listening and you know she's on your side. She's not gonna hurt you.

. . . When you're gonna merge with a company or acquire another company, it's supposed to be top secret. You have to do something to stem the rumors because it might screw up the deal. Talk of the merger, the whole place is in a turmoil. It's like somebody saying there's a bomb in the building and we don't know where it is and when it's going to go off. There've been so many mergers where top executives are laid off, the accounting department is cut by 60 per cent, the manufacturing is cut by 20 per cent. I have yet to find anybody in a corporation who was so secure to honestly believe it couldn't happen to him.

. . . As he struggles in this jungle, every position he's in, he's terribly lonely. He can't confide and talk with the guy working under him. He can't confide and talk to the man he's working for. To give vent to his feelings, his fears and his insecurities, he'd expose himself. This goes all the way up the line until he gets to be president. The president *really* doesn't have anybody to talk to, because the vice presidents are waiting for him to die or make a mistake and get knocked off so they can get his job.

He can't talk to the board of directors, because to them he has to appear as a tower of strength, knowledge, and wisdom, and have the ability to walk on water. The board of directors, they're cold, they're hard. They don't have any direct-line responsibilities. They sit in a staff capacity and they really play God. They're interested in profits. They're interested in progress. They're interested in keeping a good face in the community — if it's profitable. You have the tremendous infighting of man against man for survival and clawing to the top. Progress.

We always saw signs of physical afflictions because of the stress and strain. Ulcers, violent headaches. I remember one of the giant corporations I was in, the chief executive officer ate Gelusil by the minute. That's for ulcers. Had a private dining room with his private chef. All he ever ate was well-done steak and well-done hamburgers.

. . .A man wants to get to the top of the corporation, not for the money involved. After a certain point, how much more money can you make? In my climb, I'll be honest. Money was secondary. Unless you have tremendous demands — yachts, private airplanes — you get to a certain point, money isn't that important. It's the power, the status, the prestige. Frankly, it's delightful to be on top and have everybody calling you Mr. Ross and have a plane at your disposal and a car and a driver at your disposal. When you come to town, there's people to take care of you. When you walk into a board meeting, everybody gets up to say hello. I don't think there's any human being that doesn't love that. It's a nice feeling. But the ultimate power is in the board of directors. I don't know anybody who's free. You read in the paper about stockholders' meetings, the annual report. It all sounds so glowing. But behind the scenes, a jungle.

Maggie Holmes
— DOMESTIC

What bugs me now, since I'm on welfare, is people saying they give you the money for nothin. When I think back what we had to come through, up from the South, comin' here, the hard work we had to do. It really gets me, when I hear people . . . It do somethin' to me. I think violence.

I think what we had to work for. I used to work for $1.50 a week. This is five days a week, sometimes six. If you live in the servant quarter, your time is never off, because if they decide to have a party at night, you gotta come out. My grandmother, I remember when she used to work we'd get milk and a pound of butter. I mean this was pay. I'm thinkin' about what my poor parents worked for, gettin' nothing. What do the white think about when they think? Do they ever think about what *they* would do?

She had worked as a domestic, hotel chambermaid, and as ''kitchen help in cafes'' for the past 25 years, up North and down South. She lives with her four children.

When it come to housework, I can't do it now. I can't stand it, cause it do somethin' to my mind. They want you to clean the house, want you to wash, even the windows, want you to iron. You not supposed to wash no dishes. You ain't supposed to make no beds up. Lots of 'em try to sneak it in on you, think you don't know that. So the doorbell rings and I didn't answer to. The bell's ringin' and I'm still doin' my work. She ask me why I don't answer the bell. I say; "Do I come here to be a butler?" And I don't see myself to be no doormaid. I came to do some work and I'm gonna do my work. When you end up, you's nursemaid, you's cook. They puts all this on you. If you want a job to cleanin', you ask for just cleanin'. She wants you to do in one day what she hasn't did all year.

Now this bug me: The first thing she gonna do is pull out this damn rubber thing — just fittin' for your knees. Knee pads — like workin' in the fields, like people pickin' cotton. No mop or nothin'. That's why you find so many black women here got rheumatism in their legs, knees. When you gets on that cold floor, I don't care how warm the house is, you can feel the cold on the floor, the water and stuff. I never see nobody on their knees until I come North. In the South, they had mops. Most times, if they had real heavy work, they always had a man to come in. Washin' windows, that's a man's job. They don't think nothin' about askin' you to do that here. They don't have no feeling that that's what bothers you. I think to myself; My God, if I had somebody come and do my floors, clean up for me, I'd appreciate it. They don't say nothin' about it. Act like you haven't even done anything. They has no feelin's.

A commonly observed phenomenon: During the early evening hour, trains, crowded, predominantly by young white men carrying attache cases, pass trains headed in the opposite direction, crowded, predominantly by middle-aged black women carrying brown paper bags. Neither group, it appears, glances at the other.

We spend most of the time ridin'. You get caught goin' out from the suburbs at nighttime, man, you're really sittin' there for hours. There's nothin' movin'. You got a certain hour to meet trains. You get a transfer, you have to get that train. It's a shuffle to get in and out of the job. If you miss that train at five o'clock, what time you gonna get out that end? Sometime you don't get home till eight o'clock . . .

You don't feel like washin' your own window when you come from out there, scrubbin'. If you work in one of them houses eight hours, you gotta come home do the same thing over . . . you don't feel like . . . (sighs softly) . . . tired. You gotta come home, take care of your kids, you gotta cook, you gotta wash. Most of the time, you gotta wash for the kids for somethin' to wear to school. You gotta clean up, 'cause you didn't have time in the morning. You gotta wash and iron and whatever you do, nights. You be so tired, until you don't feel like even doin' nothin'.

You get up at six, you fix breakfast for the kids, you get them ready to go on to school. Leave home about eight. Most of the time I make biscuits for my kids, cornbread you gotta make. I don't mean the canned kind. This I don't call cookin', when you go in that refrigerator and get some beans and drop 'em in a pot. And TV dinners, they go stick 'em in the stove and she say she cooked. This is not cookin'.

And *she's* tired. Tired from doin' what? You got a washing dryer, you got an electric sweeper, anything at fingertips. All she gotta do is unfroze 'em, dump 'em in the pot, and she's tired! I go to the store, I get my vegetables, greens, I wash 'em. I gotta pick 'em first. I don't eat none of that stuff, like in the cans. She don't do that, and she says she's tired.

When you work for them, when you get in that house in the morning, boy, they got one arm in their coat and a scarf on their head. And when you open that door, she shoots by you, she's gone. Know what I mean? They want you to come there and keep the kids and let them get out. What she think about how am I gonna do? Like I gets tired of my kids too. I'd like to go out too. It bugs you to think that they don't have no feelin's about that.

Most of the time I work for them and they be out. I don't like to work for 'em when they be in the house so much. They don't have no work to do. All they do is get on the telephone and talk about one another. Make you sick. I'll go and close the door. They're all the same, everybody's house is the same. You think they rehearse it . . .

When I work, only thing I be worryin' about is my kids. I just don't like to leave 'em too long. When they get out of school, you wonder if they out on the street. The only thing I worry is if they had a place to play in easy. I always call two, three times. When she don't like you to call, I'm in a hurry to get out of there. (Laughs) My mind is gettin' home, what are you gonna find to cook before the stores close.

This Nixon was sayin' he don't see nothin' wrong with people doin' scrubbin'. For generations that's all we done. He should know we wants to be doctors and teachers and lawyers like him. I don't want my kids to come up and do domestic work. It's degrading. You can't see no tomorrow there. We done this for generation and generation — cooks and butlers all you life. They want their kids to be lawyers, doctors, and things. You don't want 'em in no cafes workin' . . .

You know what I wanted to do all my life? I wanted to play piano. And I'd want to write songs and things, that's what I really wanted to do. If I could just get myself enough to buy a piano . . . And I'd like to write about my life, if I could sit long enough: How I growed up in the South and my grandparents and my father — I'd like to do that. I would like to dig up more of black history, too. I would love to for my kids.

Lotta time I'm tellin' 'em about things, they'll be sayin', "Mom, that's olden days." (Laughs.) They don't understand, because it's so far from what's happening now. Mighty few young black women are doin' domestic work. And I'm glad. That's why I want my kids to go to school. This one lady told me, "All you people are gettin' like that." I said, "I'm glad." There's no more gettin' on their knees.

Betsy Delacy
— PATIENTS' REPRESENTATIVE

I'm called a patients' representative. My job is to admit them into the hospital. I'm the first one they see when they walk in the door and the last one to see when they leave. When they get their bills in the mail, they think of me. I think my name is listed along with the fire and police department on their telephone. (Laughs.) Who to call in emergencies.

. . .I handle patients A, B, J, and K. We call insurance companies and find out what their benefits are. Then we code the count for the computer. We type up all the necessary forms. This is called pre-admit. We let you know what your benefits are so you don't have to worry about your hospital bill. Our rooms are $75 a day. If the insurance pays only $25, that man's going to owe $50 out of his own pocket every day he's here. I get the money ahead of time. You don't have insurance, there must be a $500 deposit. You have to come walking in here with $500 if you're going to be put in bed.

When you ask for money first thing he comes in, it tends to upset the patient sometimes, unless you put it in a way that they're most grateful. I find the best way to do that, without myself being yelled at and called names, is to charm the patient and they calm down. "Are you aware of what our benefits are? Do you have the means to pay the other $50 a day?" They think you're informing them rather than demanding money. But you are demanding money.

When I visit you, I've warned you and I've joked about it. I've taken the edge off the whole thing. So it's not a big shock. I'd rather go up to you and say, "Sir, you owe $200," than not bother you and one day you walk out, and you owe $1500 and have to drop your teeth and have another heart attack. Health care is expensive, you know.

I don't feel I represent the patient. I represent the hospital. I represent the cashiers. I'm the buffer between the patient and the collection department. This job could be done with a little more finesse. There are times when we dun the patient while he's in bed: "Tomorrow, can you have $300 paid on this bill?"

. . .They want the bill explained. It's computerized, and it had taken me about three weeks to understand when I started out on this job. The patient's just looking at all these figures and doesn't know what's coming off.

Computers make it worse than before. You used to have three cashiers. You now have seven. There's the coding, there's the sorting, there's the tearing apart of pieces of paper. At one time all you had to do was write a little figure in the corner and that was it. Something very simple you used to do in five minutes now takes you five days. Hospital costs have gone up since computers. The cost of an error is so fantastic. Where if you've paid $10 and I've written down a receipt for 100, it's a simple little mistake. All I had to do was scratch out the 100 and write 10. Now if that kind of error's made, it ties everything up for five days.

. . .People see hospitals as money first and health second. On our admitting forms we ask all these questions — next of kin, who's gonna pay the bill? — and fill out all these blank squares. The *last* question is: "What is wrong with you, sir?" I'd rather see patient care first and your financial problems second.

. . .I'd like to see one insurance for all people, one plan — socialized. Free medical care would be wonderful, but I don't know how it would be supported. We'd only end up paying for it through taxes. That would tend to irritate people. Intelligent people realize health care is expensive. They realize hospitals don't make profits. Hospitals misuse money badly. But that's poor management. ∎

The Market of Human Beings

Min Chong Suk works as a sewer in Seoul, Korea's Peace Market Garment District. She is one of approximately 300,000 textile workers who have contributed to South Korea's "economic miracle," but have seen little of its fruits.

Min Chong Suk
TEXTILE WORKER

My day starts with my mother's voice waking me — "Get up! It's already 6:30." — Oh, I have to get up. I shouldn't spoil myself. But six hours sleep is too short for me. I leave my home at 7 a.m., come back around 11:30 p.m. and take a supper around midnight. This is my schedule every day.

Our room is not so small since it measures nine meters square, but one part is used for the kitchen and another part for drawers and a desk. There's not

Excerpted from a longer autobiography, entitled *The Market of Human Beings*, distributed by the American Friends Service Committee. Complete document was first published in Korean in 1977, translated into Japanese, then translated from the Japanese into English in 1978. Available from AFSC, Roberta Levenbach, 1501 Cherry St., Phila., Pa. 19102.

enough space for the seven members of our family to sleep. I have difficulty finding my place to sleep when I get back at midnight even if my mother asks my younger brothers to leave a place for me.

Seven o'clock is still somewhat dark. Walking through the barracks I can hear the noise of plates clapping which sounds so sad to me. Most of the people here live like me. They go to work early in the morning and get back late at night. Rush hour for this community's bus is seven to eight in the morning and 10 to 11 in the evening. We work longer hours than regular persons, twice as long as them. Why are we now so poor and never able to escape?

We have a strong will to have a better life. Why is our life getting worse day by day? Something must be crazy. . . .

All of the passengers on the bus are young girls around twenty years old, except for the students. We all have the same hard life. We are bound together with one string and are exploited and restrained.

Why can't we cut this dirty string? I have no idea. When people resisted in Chong Kye chon several years ago against the government policy which evicted us from our houses there, bulldozers came and took down our barracks in a minute. Poor people should be united, but how? If we were united could we make any change — with the many rich people and government officials with their money and their rights?

After a one-hour ride, the bus arrives at the factory. It looks like a jail — a brick building with only a few windows. Our working room is a big hall divided into several sections by thin wooden partitions. On the hall side there are no windows. Maybe the company doesn't want people to be able to look in. It smells of dust. Several ventilators are not enough for this large messy room with materials, sewing machines and people.

The wage system has many amazing points here: Legally the shidas (young female apprentices) should receive a monthly salary from the managers or be paid by the hours they actually worked. But the managers pay such a small amount that the sewing machine operators feel sorry and help the shidas. This means the shidas must be dependent on both the managers and the operators. They devote their bodies, hearts, growth and everything for that 8,000 won a month.

After paying transportation fees, the shidas have only enough money left for one bowl of buckwheat soup. It's amazing that their small earnings are the largest income for their families. Heran's father has left home. Her mother used to sell fish on the street to make a living, but when the road was relocated as part of the "Saemaul" movement, she lost her job. Now she earns 200-300 won per day by making envelopes at home. Other shidas' lives are similar to Heran's in this Peace Market. When I asked Heran what she wants to be in the future, she answered, "I want to be a good sewing machine operator like you."

Heran said she wanted to be a skillful sewing machine operator like me. I can understand her hope since I had the same at her age. You don't know if you don't become an operator. We have so many diseases — bronchitis, indigestion and neuralgia. Sometimes, people around me think I am tubercular when I cough too much. When the weather is bad my hip aches. Sometimes I can't open my eyes in the strong sunlight. I don't know the name of that disease. Also, our hands have many wounds from sewing. Heran, you may want to be a charming woman, but this is not the place to become attractive. Our skin turns yellow because of less chance to get sunshine. Our hands change from women's shape to men's shape. When we meet someone, we try not to show our hands, from shame. We work from 7 in the morning until 11:30 at night. We can't get enough wages and have gotten old without getting married. Heran, how can I suggest "be a good operator" to you? I should pray that you don't become one — pray that you could give this up and start a new life. But here I am teaching you how to become an operator. I may be an irresponsible person. I don't know myself. I know I am not trying to cheat you. I take care of you. But, in spite of our hopes, everyone here has no way to leave, so we have to learn to be good sewers.

I wonder if this is our destiny. Is poverty a sin, or is someone keeping us poor? Something must be wrong. Even if we work a whole day, we don't get paid for all the hours. If the manager asks us to do something, we just do it. We are ignorant and lazy.

Is ignorance a sin? No matter how our skills improve, no matter how hard we work, our lives have not been changed. The reality is the opposite. Life is becoming worse here day by day. Yet we don't have any idea how to avoid this.

The decay of public morals in this Peace Market can't be avoided. Ten years ago, when there were many houses of ill fame in Chong Kye chon and Change shin Dong, a lot of young girls who came from the countryside and had trouble making a living drifted here. These people entered factories and worked as shidas and then as operators. But their wages were terribly low and they had no place to live. They slept leaning against the wall in the hallway near the entrance to the factory. Finally almost all of these girls had to go to the amusement section of town. They made clothes in the daytime, and stayed in unpermitted lodgings at night selling their bodies. Otherwise they couldn't support themselves.

How come it is so hard to live as this? Is it really such a hard thing to have three meals a day? Do people have to sell their bodies even to live, I wonder. No. To live should not be like that. The reason we are poor like this is that the owners have been exploiting us. In spite of economic development or modernization of our homeland, our pain has not been changed at all. I feel angry when someone says that people can make a living easier these days.

Work is an important thing to one's life. To eat good food and to play with pleasure should be combined with this. Work, which is basic, should be our greatest pleasure. Instead, we live such a painful life. We must sell our labor. It would be all right if we were paid fair wages, but we are not.

People have said recently that our government is spending money recklessly in the United States, England, Switzerland and maybe Japan. Some king of an African country deposited a big amount of money in a bank in Switzerland. I hope powerful people in our country are not doing this. Anyone who felt free to do this should visit the Peace Market to look at us. How do they explain their using foreign goods, such as watches, glasses, ties, shoes and their wives' clothes? Even the decorations of their houses, the plants in their gardens, and the goldfish in their ponds are all foreign. If they like foreign goods so much, they had better migrate to a foreign country. But I know they won't do it. Because they wouldn't be able to exploit the workers as they do here.

The people who are called economic scholars use "international competition" or some other difficult phrase when they talk. But we know they mean a way to squeeze workers' flesh and blood. Seen from this point of view, well-educated people are not always humane. According to Ms. Chong, some scholars have said that inflation can't be avoided for economic growth. What are they pursuing "economic growth" for? Inflation means the lowering of workers' wages and consumers being exploited. And if "economic growth" consists of the exploitation of people including workers, it isn't necessary to grow economically. They simply disregard our hard life. I was surprised by Ms. Chong's explanation. People who lead, like scholars, are standing on the side of officials and owners.

To judge something is difficult. The same truth looks different depending on where you stand. The scholars should stand on the side of the people in looking at export and economic development. People can't feel our pain without standing on our side. The only ones who can see and think from our point of view are ourselves. Only we know the pain. I feel that it is true that workers' rights will have to be acquired by workers. ∎

Working People Who Can't Find Work

Rosie Washington

Unemployed and on welfare, 27; in the small apartment she shares with her daughter, 6, and another woman, from which they are about to be evicted.

You look in the paper, see all these jobs in Cheektowaga, Williamsville; no way to get to them, bus don't even go that way. You go up and go looking for a job; the jobs they send you to, 50 per cent of the time there's not a job anyway. "Well, we're not hiring now, but we'll take your application." Then they send you out to jobs that they know you're either overqualified for or underqualified for. I was an administrative assistant at a community center; I've been an employment coach on a Federal program, then a counselor. I've done all this, and I really like it. But my biggest problem is that I don't have that piece of paper that says I'm qualified, so now, well, I went to the restaurants, hotels, plants. I've said I never wanted to work in any plant. I wish I could get a plant job now — I have applications in at Bethlehem, Chevy, Ford. You can't get any answers, you can't get any services, just sit around and wait, just to be told to come back and go through it again. Honest to God.

And the welfare system. Isn't that a design, a design to fail? They just give you enough money so you don't starve to death, so you're always hungry. They don't give you enough to live, just to exist. You know, I think these clerks, they look at me as an imposition on their paychecks. They're paying for me: "If it wasn't for her, I might have a nickel or a dime more." But you know, they want us here. They always got to have somebody on the bottom, so they know they're closer to the top. A crummy welfare recipient chewing up their tax dollar, you dig it? With me here, I can make you feel better. . . .

I'm tired. I really am. I have a child, and she's part

of me. She sees me doing nothing, never going out to work, depressed, worried, sometimes crying. I mean, I try. I try to play with her. When I have some money, we even go out together. We can't afford the movies, but I take her to Henry's and buy her a hamburger. I do love her. I do care, but with all the pressure, sometimes I can't even talk to her — you know. She comes home: "Hi, Mommy." "Hi, how was school today?" "Fine." She wants to play, but I

The New York Times Magazine, February 12, 1975.

20

can't. I think it's going to affect her emotionally. I went to school with her and the teacher said, "She's a good, bright child, but she's so sad. Why?" I said, "Because that's all we got in our home. Sadness. No hope. No future."

And this country thinks it's so damn great. It's *not*. It's hard to believe, but I really feel we're going to have a revolution, because this government ain't doing it, not to say any other kind is better. What I'd like to know, really, is what am I supposed to do with my life? I had my goals, but no means to make them. I'm just at the breaking point. And when I break, what am I going to do? You're just never right for anything. At first you're too young; then you don't have experience; by the time you're 35 to 40 years, you're too old. So all through your life you were never right for anything. You know, it's everything — job and experience — no experience, no job. To get a job you gotta have money; you gotta have a job to get money. So it's just a vicious circle of nothing. And you're all locked up in this thing, crossed in it all your life. One circle that leads nowhere. That makes you pretty angry. Angry isn't even the word for it. I don't even *know* how to describe that feeling.

Alfred Prato

Unemployed laborer, laid off from the New York City Parks Department. [Story told by *The New York Times*.]

Sometimes at night, after another lonely disappointment-filled day, Alfred Prato will try to still the apprehensions in his household by letting the children climb into bed with him and Marie for a few minutes.

They hug and say how much they love one another.

But sometimes that is not enough to overcome the anxieties of the Pratos' eldest son, 7-year-old Anthony, who hears the talk about the mortgage, the cost of food and the lack of a job.

"He's worried," said Mr. Prato the other day. "He expects to wake up and find us out in the street."

When Anthony starts asking, "What's going to happen to us?" Mr. Prato wraps his arms about his son and roughhouses a bit with him. "I tell him, 'You concentrate on being a little boy; you don't have to worry about grown-up stuff yet.' "

Mr. Prato is 30 years old and lives on Staten Island. He is one of an estimated 20,000 New York City employees who have lost their jobs this year as

the result of budget cuts.

For 10 years, Mr. Prato was a proud laborer for the city Parks Department. He made $12,000 a year, owned a 1972 Chevrolet Nova automobile for which he paid $2,600 cash and he and his wife bought a small ranch-style house.

Last June, along with 500 other park laborers, Mr. Prato was laid off.

He is no longer proud.

"SHE IS MY STRENGTH"

Alfred Prato is unsure of himself. After more than 20 job interviews, he has not had an offer.

He worries constantly.

"It's with you 24 hours a day," he said. "When I got laid off, I weighed 172 pounds. Now I weigh 157."

Mr. Prato was born in Manhattan. His mother died when he was born. The aunt who raised him now lives in Italy. His father has remarried and lives at Port Richey, Fla.

When he was a student at Chelsea Vocational High School, Mr. Prato went to Coney Island one day with a "couple of my friends" and there he met Marie, a red-haired girl who was born in Italy.

They were married in September 1965. In November of that year he was hired by the Parks Department and he has worked there ever since.

Five months of job hunting has left Mr. Prato with nervous trembling in his fingers and the beginnings of a facial tic. He feels that he might disintegrate, were it not for his wife.

"She is a good woman," he said. "She is my strength. She keeps me going. She tells me that someday I'll walk into a place and get a job. She's sure of it."

When Mr. Prato was a little boy, growing up under the guidance of his thrift-conscious aunt from Italy, he was constantly urged, "Make something of yourself."

He and Marie refused to live on credit after they married. She worked for Metropolitan Life until she was eight months pregnant with Anthony, and they saved their money to buy a house.

"EVERYTHING WAS FINE"

"Everything was just fine," said Mr. Prato, sitting with his wife in soft lamplight at evening, playing with the new baby, Dominick, while Anthony struggled with his first-grade readers.

"Then came June; everything just ended," Mr. Prato said. "We had a little money saved. We cashed in my insurance policy."

He applied for unemployment benefits and gets $95 a week. "I'm eligible until next July," he said.

For a time after he was laid off, Mr. Prato tried to do some unpaid union work, going to Albany to help

THE LATEST WHITE HOUSE LINE ON RISING UNEMPLOYMENT

UNEMPLOYED

lobby through the General Assembly a special appropriation of $330 million. When that became law, 235 of the park laborers were rehired. Mr. Prato was 255th on the seniority list.

When it became evident that there was little likelihood that he would get his city job back soon, Mr. Prato began a serious search for work.

"I went to the unemployment center," he said. "I wasn't even interviewed. The woman there wrote on my application, 'Come back Jan. 26.'

"I remember one day the United States Public Health Service hospital on Staten Island was hiring. Marie and I both went down. I said I would take any job. The hospital said they had 50 teachers that came in to look for menial work. That got to me — all those well-educated people who couldn't find jobs.

"I heard about an opening at another place. We got up early. My wife said, 'Don't be nervous, you'll do fine.' When I got there, there were 50 guys waiting for the job. What bothered me was that I'm 30 years old and I was the oldest guy there.

"My wife saw an ad in the paper for a girl. They were giving interviews on Monday and Tuesday. My wife got dressed up to go to apply for it. I told her to telephone first because it was a holiday. She did. The girl who answered the phone said, 'I already got the job.'

"At the unemployment center, the lines are running out the doors. It's really pathetic. Firemen, policemen, laborers, teachers — decent people who put a lot of time and energy in their jobs.

"I had 10 years with the city. Those are 10 years blown away. I'm put on the preferred list for four years. If I don't get called back, forget it.

"Nobody really cares. Politicians don't care. The people who are supposed to represent you don't care. You don't hear nothing from them, the President, the Governor, the Mayor, the Senators. They're playing games. We are pawns. They are playing with our lives."

A FEELING OF HELPLESSNESS

The Pratos, with the help of their savings, are almost able to handle the mechanics of living. They eat a lot of macaroni. Mrs. Prato saves an estimated $4 a week on foods by using coupons clipped from newspapers. The Pratos do not drink, smoke or entertain. On Fridays Mr. Prato's older brother comes over and brings a cake for the children.

Mr. Prato is sometimes tempted to stop trying, to sit back and let the future wash over him.

"The worst thing, I guess, that could happen to someone is when someone you love dies," he said. "The next-worst thing is for a man to lose his job."

He said that some nights after everybody else in the family has gone to bed, he takes a final check of his sleeping sons.

"I stand there looking at them and thinking. 'I brought them into the world, and I can't even provide for them.' You feel like a failure. Less than a man." ∎

Group Exercise

After the stories have been read, the facilitator will ask each participant to talk to the group about the person(s) in his/her story. The following questions can serve as guides:

1 Give a personal and social description of the person about whom you read.

2 What kinds of things do they complain about or feel most oppressed by?

3 In what ways do they exhibit resistance to forces of alienation and oppression?

4 What do they dream about?

5 How would work have to be reorganized if these workers' dreams were to be fulfilled?

When all members of the group have finished with the description of their *worker*, the facilitator will ask the group to list on a sheet of newsprint or on a chalk board the common themes and major differences among the stories they heard.

Keeping those themes and differences before the group, the facilitator will then ask each person to talk about their own work life, using the following questions as guides.

1 Where do you work? In what sector of the economy and for whom? What do you do?

2 How is your workplace organized? Who makes decisions? Who occupies what space? What is the ethnic and sexual division of labor? What are the rewards, differences in status, that are offered?

3 Who does the product or service you are producing benefit the most?

4 What do you like about your job? What is most frustrating, alienating or oppressive about it?

5 What would you like to change in your workplace? What are *your* extraordinary dreams?

6 Who in your workplace shares outlooks like your own? Who does not share your concerns and problems?

After everyone has told his/her story, the facilitator will ask the group to put a check mark beside each of the themes common to both the participants and the people whose stories they read.

The session should close with the group listing on newsprint or chalk board what they think prevents work life from being reorganized in the ways desired by workers.

We Make History...
Or It Makes Us

In Session One we looked at our work experiences and began to ask questions about alienation. As we listened and told our own stories to each other we noticed that working conditions have not always remained the same. Even in our lifetime, some of us have moved from a more creative work experience to one in which we have less control. Others have moved from a brutal work experience to less overtly repressive working conditions.

To understand why work is organized as it is, it is necessary not only to tell our individual stories, but also to place them in their historical context to understand them in relation to the system which determines the overall pattern of work under capitalist organization. Only when we begin to get a handle on how our system works and what our point of leverage is within it, can we possibly think of changing it. Otherwise, we are likely to remain locked into a fatalistic world view merely trying to make the best out of a bad situation.

One of the myths which has prevented workers from acting collectively to change their conditions is that of *upward social mobility*. There is a common assumption in this country that people start off with the same opportunities and end up with different status and in different economic brackets simply because they are lazy or inept or without the *proper* educational background or mental ability needed to make it. Those who succeed are often judged smarter, more clever or luckier than others. True, we recognize the influence of racial and sexual discrimination in preventing people from getting the kind of status, autonomy or economic success that capitalism promises. But racism and sexism are usually seen as aberrations of an otherwise fair system which, if eliminated, would allow everyone the equal access promised by the American Dream. In an attempt to explain this myth and the real dynamics of capitalism in such a way as to enable us to locate ourselves within the changing structure of our economy, we have chosen the following articles by Frank Cunningham and William Tabb.

Frank Cunningham demonstrates that at the heart of our economic system lies a fundamental antagonism between those who must *work* in order to survive and those who *own* the productive resources upon which all depend. This fundamental *class* difference (between workers and owners) is the main social contradiction from which other forms of inequality develop.

William Tabb extends Cunningham's thesis into an examination of the specific changes through which capitalism has passed, bringing us to the present period of transition and its effect on workers, consumers and the environment. Tabb's presentation sheds further light on the conditions described in the first session of this course.

These two articles provide the background for our own family and class histories. The "hidden injuries of class" (as Richard Sennett and Jonathan Cobb have entitled their well-known study of white, blue-collar workers in Boston) is one of the best kept secrets in America. It is important for Christians to understand how we are all shaped by our location in the present class stratification if we are to work for a society in which there will be no such distinctions.

The article by Sheila Collins provides us with an example of one person's attempt to understand her background in terms of the pervasive reality of class and the response (or rather, lack of it) of churches to this reality. ∎

Class, Family, Forgiveness

by Sheila Collins

The last memory I have of my father is the slow-motion image of him caught at the corner of my vision through the dining room window as he sank to the ground in front of our house, his great bulk toppling like a skyscraper in an earthquake, or like some giant sequoia, perched at 90 degrees before the final plummet. He would have like the comparison with a felled tree, for his heart was in the northern Canadian woods, and his best paintings were always of lumbermen and trappers — those rugged individualists who, because they were bound to the land, still knew about connections.

My father would live three years beyond this first evidence we had of his blighted heart, but from that time on he knew that we were now aware of what had been going on within him all those years. It takes a long time to build up a residue of sludge in the arteries. The heart does not easily give up its prerogatives. Beauty, love, trust, dignity, honor, solidarity with other living creatures are only gradually squeezed out of the vessels and replaced with more deadly substances: Uniformity, competition, caricature, humiliation, suspicion.

Perhaps it is dignity that is the last to go — that quality of self-deceit which insists that we are "somebody" long after the institutions around us have defined us as ciphers. An Appalachian woman, transplanted to a poverty-ridden neighborhood in Chicago, told a friend of mine recently: "We still have our dignity. Without your dignity, you lose your life."

My father was a proud man — too proud to cry out in the New York commuter train crowded with homebound businessmen when that first icy grip constricted his chest and he realized he was about to become the victim of a disease he had dreaded all his life. It shamed him. He could not admit to my mother what was wrong, as he got cold and sweating into bed that night. His collapse in the front yard a few

months later was the first indication that we had that he was suffering from a broken heart.

I always saw my father's life as a tragedy of the unfulfilled. He died at the age of 52, never having realized his dream of becoming a fine painter and a published author. There was little that I can recall of pure joy in his life; little pleasure. His life was lived trying to keep his family out of debt. The tangible achievements were meager: A few third-rate children's books "illustrated by E. Joseph Dreany" and a sheaf of crude, done-to-order tempera paintings of macho men, dressed alternatively as cowboys, biblical heroes or American Presidents, who always seemed to be positioned in various poses of dominance, authority or coercion over cowgirls, biblical heroines or First Ladies all looking like Vivien Leigh's Scarlett.

Besides the illustrations, there are a few watercolors suggestive of real artistic power. They are Depression-era scenes of houses and churches, perched like cormorants on the rugged outcroppings overlooking a vast inland sea characteristic of the northern Ontario mining country from which he came. Or they are of people engaged in struggle against the elements (most likely immigrants from Ireland or Eastern Europe): Women hanging out wash on a windy day against a backdrop of fierce sky and black rock, or men with axes, shovels and traps in various acts of thrusting, digging and lifting. All the anguish and exhilaration of the historical battle to domesticate nature are suggested in these paintings, which I have decided are my father's greatest bequest to his children. Like the few African words Kunta Kinte passed down to his children, these paintings preserve the feel and time of a culture those of us who have "made it" in America have sought to erase from memory. Perhaps because it was too raw, too revealing of the darker side of the American reality?

A POWER DIMINISHED

Had he not had to worry about financial security, my father might have been the Edward Hooper of the Canadian industrial frontier, or the Canadian James Agee, recording with outrageous love the

Sheila Collins works with the National Division of the Board of Global Ministries, United Methodist Church. Reprinted from the April 17, 1978 issue of *Christianity and Crisis*, Copyright © 1978 by Christianity and Crisis, Inc.

silent sorrows of those miners, shopkeepers and woodsmen who flocked to the Canadian wilderness in search of a better life, and very often found there poverty, disease and exploitation. A few cherished paintings — not even enough to fill a gallery or a retrospective book — to indicate the thwarted genius of my father.

Recently, my mother, a portrait painter, called to tell me of the exhibition of 200 years of women's art which she had just seen at the Brooklyn Museum. She shared with me her outrage that so much genius should have been buried in museum basements for

centuries, simply because the paintings were done by women and females were not supposed to be possessed of genius. My mother and I have been commiserating together like this for some time now, ever since the women's movement gave her a language that legitimized her lifelong battle with sexist roles, and gave me the code to unlock her aberrant behavior as a parent. The movement was the vehicle of my being able to forgive her.

If feminism gave us a shared language, reconciling at last the old antagonisms between mother and daughter, it is only as I have come to understand the nature of class in America that I have been able to comprehend the special obsessions and sadness of my father's life. Perhaps if there had been a mass-based socialist movement in this country to focus and define class-based anger, perhaps if I had been educated at an earlier age about the history of working-class struggles, Dad and I would at least have had a vocabulary in which to communicate. (As it is, this history has mostly been a process of self-education, through digging out books and pamphlets generally not available through established channels, or through talking with older people who remember.) He died before my education began, and so the burdens he carried festered in the hothouse of individual guilt and neurosis. Turned in upon the self, his passions killed him year by year.

Freudians would have had a time with my father! Bereft of his own father in infancy, raised by an obsessive-compulsive mother and a maiden aunt who supported her sister's child through nursing — a boy raised to "wear the pants" in the family, but with a woman's instincts for nurturance and beauty — he became a compulsive worrier, obsessed with the fear of destitution.

Thank goodness we never had the money, and to some extent therefore the necessity, for psychotherapy. There is much in psychoanalysis that could plausibly explain my father's neurosis, or, more accurately, explain the mechanism by which a neurosis becomes embedded in the human character structure. Most psychoanalysts, however, would have misdiagnosed the source of my father's neurosis. Freud did not look past the presenting symptoms of his own bourgeois culture. There are deeper things to be said about the formation of the human personality. They are lodged in that often unacknowledged web of social and economic relations in which the family is situated, and in the effect of particular skies, rocks, trees, rivers, plains, dwellings on the developing aesthetic of the young child. I doubt that psychoanalysis could have cured my father. Perhaps only a revolution could have saved his life — but then, the artistic spirit has had a habit of rebelling against the inevitable fetters of almost any social system.

To understand my father's gifts and his grief, I have had to go back to the earliest memories I have of Copper Cliff, the nickel and copper mining town in northern Ontario where he was born. I must have been a child of about four when I visited my grandmother there, before she and her sister moved to the center of the mining region in Sudbury. Of all the places I visited when I was young, the town of Copper Cliff stands out vividly in my memory as an environment of unrelenting harshness. I can still see the mud streets and plank sidewalks, the little frame houses sitting like orphans on the windy flats, and over it all the great smokestacks and rumbling conveyor belts bringing ore to the mills to be crushed and refined. I can still see the pall of yellow air that hung over the town and the giant slag heaps like pyramids rising out of the desert, monuments to the wastefulness of industrial progress. Agnes Smedley's recollections of her childhood in the mining camps of the American southwest which she describes in *Daughter of Earth* (a book lost to the reading public until recently resurrected by the Feminist Press) have strong resonances in my own memories of Copper Cliff.

SURVIVAL AND STRESS

Freud would not have asked how a woman, widowed with a young baby, could have been expected to support herself in towns like this. He would have attributed the compulsive attention to cleanliness to anal fixation, and the obsessive cold pride and guardedness to frigidity and sexual repression. He would not have asked how it was possible to raise a child to be secure and self-actualized when the only jobs available were in the mines and those open only to men, when there was no Social Security, Medicaid or welfare to ease the burdens of poverty; no television to anesthetize the mind.

They survived, I suppose, as most poor women did — by taking in washing, letting out rooms, growing food in backyard plots, and making do until another breadwinner came along in the person of a railroad clerk who married my grandmother when my father was in high school. My father went out as soon as he was old enough to clerk in a store, running errands for the stationmaster, adding to the little pot from which all survived. I know that is how they made it, and knowing that makes me fearful for my generation and the next; for the ability of people to construct their survival in the interstices of the market system has been eroded since then. The penetration of conglomerates into almost every area of our lives, coupled with the urbanization and atomization of the family has obliterated opportunities for the little entrepreneurial activities on which the poor formerly depended in times of crisis. To be sure, the welfare state has made up for the gap, but it has been at the expense of the control the poor once had over their survival. The result is a diminution in their ability to feed one another. The loaves and fishes can no longer be multiplied. Without money to purchase them from the supermarket, there are few miracles left.

As soon as he was 16, my father emigrated to Toronto in search of work as an artist. As a child, he had forever doodled, and his cartoons of his class-mates and teachers can still be seen in the high school yearbooks. He was a pacific man, unsuited to the rough-and-tumble of life on the frontier.

My father and mother met on a picket line during an artists' strike organized by Communists. My mother, who grew up in a high school chemistry teacher's family and had graduated from the Ontario College of Art, was working at the time as a fashion illustrator for one of the big Toronto papers. Though the work had sounded glamorous, she found it as boring and alienating as many factory jobs, and as poorly paid. My father, picking up jobs wherever he could, was designing egg cartons and cigarette boxes at the time of the strike.

The union organizing effort was eventually broken through red-baiting, and my parents' initial flirtation with political activism came to an end, though this event was the beginning of a long and fateful relationship between the two of them.

After their marriage, my father took the only kind of art work he could find that would pay him a steady income. He did illustrations for a series of pulp magazines. In a more innocent age, these maga-zines were the precursors of modern *Playboy*, *Pent-house* and *Screw*. They contained tales of macho der-ring-do: Encounters with Indians, who of course were always portrayed as bloodthirsty savages, or tales of high adventure at sea. If there was not an adoring female in the story, he was told to work her into the illustration anyway. In my recollection, these drawings were always of scenes of violence with a pretty, buxom woman cowering in the corner of the picture, her eyes popping and hands upraised in fright as "her man" got his enemy with a knife or garrote. In my photo collection are several pictures of my mother (who, for as long as I can remember always wore pants) dressed sometimes in a bouffant skirt, at other times in bathing suit, posed in these uncharacteristic postures. Later on, I step self-con-sciously into my mother's skirts and my younger brother becomes the man to whom I must look up, for we all had to serve, at times, as my father's models in the family economy of the working class.

With her first child on the way, my mother quit work at the newspaper to try to begin a career as a portrait painter, work she could do at home. Though she had always wanted to paint portraits, she was nevertheless forced into doing it at a pace and under conditions hardly conducive to the development of fine art. She began by painting her neighbors in the room that doubled as her bedroom on the second floor of a small house; the first floor my parents had to sublet in order to get enough money to pay the rent. Soon, amidst baby squalls and bangs on the floor from the temperamental invalid who rented the rooms below, she had developed a clientele beyond the neighborhood and was contributing equally to the family budget.

LIFE IN SEGMENTS

I have few memories of my father during this time. He was the one who left early in the morning and returned only at night. My mother and her work were a part of the taste and sounds and smells of my early childhood. Turpentine and linseed oil mixed with the smells of talcum powder and turnips. It was all of a piece, my mother's "work" and her life. My father — like most men — was the one whose life was separated into compartments labeled "father" and "artist" or "wage-earner,"with the former role getting the short end of the stick. I remember visiting my father once at his place of employment — a dingy little office peopled by cigar-chomping men and plastered with girlie pictures.

When I was about six, my father left one morning and didn't return to the house on Glenlake Avenue. The market for commercial art was drying up in Toronto, and he had gone to the United States to look for work. As I learned years later, he found a room for $5 a week in New Rochelle, N.Y., where I now live, and looked for jobs for several months before getting one. For a year and a half my mother was the sole support of the family, juggling canvases, portrait subjects and children in her upstairs bed-room. In the winter, she tells me, the temperature did not go above 40 degrees, and baths were taken in a wash-pan in front of the gas stove.

She survived that period as so many before and after her have done, through the network of women in that urban working-class community who were al-ways willing to take another child into their homes or to rush over with a fully-prepared meal when their neighbor was in trouble. In addition, her own mother lived only a few blocks away and it was my grand-mother who was the functional mother in my early years.

Though these arrangements seemed at the time to be the way life was arranged everywhere, it occurs to me now how little credit the dominant value system in our society, or in our churches, has given to these informal networks of women — networks which throughout the period of industrialization have

meant the difference between a family's survival and disintegration. To the extent that families in the *barrios* and *favelas* of Latin America, in the Bantustans of South Africa or the ghettoes of New York or Los Angeles are able to survive, it is because of the mutual support provided by such networks among the suffering. When my husband and I worked in a black and Puerto Rican neighborhood in East Harlem in the '60s, I was always amazed at the food produced for the weekly church dinners. The best potluck meals in the world came out of the kitchens of poor women! It is here, rather than at the altar, that the spirit of communion is truly understood. In a sense, such communities of support, now rapidly being destroyed, are the early Christian community at work, without liturgy or ritual, dividing up the loaves and fishes, giving according to each as each has need.

Perhaps it was because of this experience of mutual interdependence that my mother survived the insecurity of trying to earn a living doing free-lance work in a competitive, commodified society with her heart intact. For although at many times in her life she has been close to penury, she has never doubted the ability of God to sustain her. And God, miraculously, has come through — in the form of money owed her which she had forgotten about, or people dropping in with gifts or skills at a time when she needed them.

Jean Baker Miller, author of *Toward a New Psychology of Women*, has pointed out that a central feature of women's development is the context in which they establish and maintain ties to others. This capacity for affiliation has been downgraded in a culture dominated by men and by the competitive market system, but it may be, she feels, one of the characteristics needed in the long run for survival. In a world bristling with engines of "defense," we can no longer afford to see the Other as an object, either to be dominated or to contend with.

THE VULNERABLE MALE

The injuries of class are hardest on men. Thrown out into the competition of the commercial marketplace, denied by masculine culture a mutually-supportive community of peers, and socialized to think of himself as a failure if he could not adequately support his family, my father early on developed the symptoms of that disease that was later to kill him. His overriding compulsion, compounded now by monthly mortgage payments that had to be met on a house in Stamford, Conn., was to produce in order to keep the family solvent. Since his work was freelance — with the advent of television he had graduated from illustrating pulp magazines to children's Little Golden Books and pop-up Stories from the Bible — he could never be certain from one month to the next if the mortgage payments could be made. Often he would work for two or three months at a time on a series of illustrations, only to have them turned down by one of the large New York publishing houses. I can remember him often, returning from a day in New York with his large portfolio under his arm, a diminished man, humiliated by some editor who had criticized the placement of a hand, the shading on a woman's neck. What did these editors know of the private grief of a man whose drawings they had summarily dismissed? They were simply fulfilling the requirements of their jobs. Production was the name of the game and there were plenty of other artists all competing for the same little slice of the pie. Through booms as well as busts, the labor market for artists, in my father's experience, always seemed to favor the buyer.

Year after year the disease got worse. Debilitated by the constant anxiety of personal inadequacy — the dominant mode of self-apprehension among men in a class-stratified society which yet appears permeable — my father became more and more irritable, harassed and despondent. His worry grew into an obsession. Most of the arguments between my father and mother erupted over money. They always ended with his shouting at her. "Well, somebody in this house has to worry about the bills!" and my mother collapsing in the tears that were her strength. Soon my father's body conformed to the obsession, his shoulders becoming rounded, his wide chest, the symbol of manliness and pride, curving into a hollow.

Yet in all those years I never saw him cry, never saw him admit to the futility etched into his body, never saw him get angry at anyone or anything else except at members of the family as a kind of reflex, for he was a gentle and loving man. The brunt of his rage was turned in upon himself. In a society in which advancement and economic success appear to depend on merit, and respect hinges on advancement, to fail is to doubt the integrity of the self.

My father made up for the lack of esteem granted him by the world by infusing his time with productivity. He would work so long and so hard that no one could accuse him of not caring. And if the time he spent working did not issue in a socially valued product — that is, one that brought in an income — then at least time itself was quantifiable, and in capitalist societies quantity sometimes makes up for quality. Thus the sacrifice of his time for his family became the measure of his love for us. And even though we begged him to take a vacation or to go on a sketching trip as he had loved to do earlier in his life, his excuse was always that he couldn't afford the time. Time had become a commodity which was purchased with his life. How ironic that those pieces of art on which my father could afford to spend least time — those paintings of the Depression and the country he loved — should now be his most valuable legacy to us.

In the center of one of these paintings, which now hangs in our living room, priests in white and gold robes followed by acolytes bearing bright red banners in commemoration of some long-dead saint parade through the middle of a town, past a flock of drably garbed onlookers. Dwarfing this human tableau rises the menacing shadow of the slag heap. For me, this painting is symbolic of the church's failure to consider the socio-economic context of its parishioners as the locus for a prophetic witness to the liberating, life-filled message of the gospel. Surrounded by conditions of human alienation and deprivation not terribly different from those in which Jesus ministered and taught, it too often offers a spectator pageant rather than a call to engagement with the concrete economic and political structures that are at the root of the powerlessness it must minister to.

Every Sunday my father attended a small, working-class Methodist church, though without the same enthusiasm he gave to his one indulgence: He was a silent movie buff who, along with a small coterie who met regularly at the Metropolitan Museum of Art, thrilled to the images of violent birth in D.W. Griffith and to the undaunted resilience of the Little Tramp. I wonder whether these movies did not strike a resonance in him about the power of class, economic suffering and struggle as social realities in a way that the pious references to guilt and suffering that he heard on Sundays — abstractions and generalities which applied to everyone and thus to no one — did not. For the church my father attended could not deal with the pain that was most central to my childhood. Unable to accept the injuries of class as a social reality in the lives of its parishioners, understanding only existential angst, not economic suffering, the church was unable to point to a vision of the Kingdom beyond the parameters of the socio-economic order in which it was embedded, or to offer a hope that was palpable. The forgiveness that must precede *metanoia* could not be mediated because there was no recognition of the real dimensions of sin.

LOVE AND POWER

Richard Sennett and Jonathan Cobb, in their book *The Hidden Injuries of Class*, indict an economic system that separates love from power:

> Once a divorce is effected between love and demonstration of power, what is the strength of love itself? Strong feelings, to be sure, but family love is also a matter of all sorts of actions in a world where power shapes experience, in which mere love does not feed the children or get the money for the vacation. Although the sense of "I" as different from my ability wards off a feeling of being only a role in the institution, it may leave a man with a sense that his capacity to love gives him no power to deal with the rest of the world. The real me who cares, the real me who is sensitive, becomes a vulnerable creature: Emotions are an area of self to be shielded, not to be expressed, lest by exposure to the world these tender spots be bruised or hurt.

By and large, the churches have been careful to maintain a separation between love and power by not challenging the political-economic sphere where power is allowed to rule, with the love ethic they cherish for the private sphere. In failing to challenge this separation, they unwittingly reinforce a system of unequal classes which, ironically, is maintained by the ideology of equality. If we are said to start from a common fund of equality and actually end up unequal, it must be because of our differing abilities, motivations and initiative.

Sennett and Cobb trace the functioning of the idea of equality as a reinforcer of the class system to the mistake of the Enlightenment thinkers who, in banishing the courts of appeal beyond the world — that is, in doing away with the sacred cosmos — eliminated a standard of human worth that could not be touched by the vicissitudes of cultural value systems.

What we need, they maintain, is an image of human dignity without a face.

Perhaps it is this appeal to a higher order — the churches' insistence on God's unconditional love — however inadequately it has been conveyed, that kept my father a Christian all those years and that keeps the people coming back to the little church in which I grew up. Such an appeal seems to be enough to keep one going amidst the assaults of an indifferent and sometimes hostile world. But is it enough to save us? Is this really the Word made flesh?

Deep in the self of each person, beneath each of the images we have created for ourselves, is an image of

human dignity, which is always the last thing to be given up. It was this dignity that Jesus was able to call upon in each of His acts of healing. Beneath all of the outward labels — pariah, female, tax collector, sinner, leper, demon-possessed — was the simple faith that to be human is to be entitled to something better than either the world's set of values or one's own neurosis or psychosis is able to offer. Often it is not until we have been stripped of most of the outward, socially-constructed vestiges of status, prestige and power, that we are able to touch this deeper source of dignity and human purpose. In the words "Your faith has made you well," Jesus names and calls forth this deeper conviction of dignity.

As Christians perhaps our task is to take back from God the power we gave over to Deity to confer human dignity on persons in the abstract, by naming and calling forth the demons which possess us — those images of class, race and gender-based power that keep us from recognizing the dignity of our common humanness. The solution is not an image of dignity without a human face but with an all too human face — the face that Jesus gave to dignity when He allied Himself with the outcasts, the women, the poor and the oppressed.

To call forth such demons, however, it to confront a monstrous power, for the institutions of racism, sexism and capitalism, both within and without us, do not yield without a battle; and it is precisely because the battle will be so fierce that we are afraid of waging it. And so we are burdened with a great

unforgiving, unable to taste the joy that comes with real forgiveness.

My father died of a broken heart, though it was diagnosed by the medical profession as "myocardial infarction." In the end, he chose dignity over life. Refusing to submit to the indignity of a bedpan, he collapsed and died in the hospital corridor on his way to the bathroom.

Upon learning of his death, my initial response was anger at being abandoned in a world without financial security. The father whom I had counted upon to carry that weight for me had admitted his own mortality. The time of reckoning had come.

A few months later, I dreamt about him. It was one of those dreams in which one is convinced that the unconscious is sending us a message. In the dream, my father was beginning a new life as the father of a young, recently married couple. He was supremely happy for the first time in his life. He was no longer *my* father, but someone else's father, fulfilling a role he had been prevented from enjoying by the compulsions of an economic system which defines "father" as "breadwinner," "provider," "strong," "silent," "master." I knew then that the process of forgiveness had begun. ∎

Toward a New Model
of Accumulation
by William Tabb

I want to talk about how capitalism has evolved over the last couple of hundred years and where it's likely to go in order to get some sense of where we come from, where we might be going and how we can intervene in that process in a creative way. First, let's look at the historical development of capitalism.

HISTORICAL ANALYSIS

1776 is a famous date to economists not because of the U.S. Declaration of Independence, but because that was the year Adam Smith wrote *The Wealth of Nations*. In that book, Smith gave a positive view of capitalism and the market. He saw it as a revolutionary change from the old ways of doing things. The market, by giving maximal freedom, would enable society to put selfishness in the common interest. This is the so-called invisible hand. It is not through the generosity of the butcher, the baker, and the candlestick maker that you get your dinner and lights on the table, but it is through their self-interest — that is, they want to make a buck. If you don't like the wares of one bakery, you go to another, and because there are many producers, many choices, the

William Tabb is an economist teaching at Queens College, New York City, and a member of the Union of Radical Political Economists. The above is a speech given at a conference of Theology in the Americas, June 1978.

consumer would get the best product at the lowest price. Before Smith, the Kings of Europe would grant monopolies to the royal favorites who would give you lousy products at high prices so that Adam's view of the market and competition was a progressive thing. Our question today is what happened to it over 200 years, since many of us certainly don't feel quite that way today.

That brings us to the question of the accumulation process. If we begin in 1776 in the United States, something like four-fifths of the labor force, (and here we're talking about the free labor force, excluding the slaves who were already in America) were property owners and professionals, farmers, artisans, crafts people, ministers, lawyers, some small manufacturers, that is, people who worked directly and produced their own livelihood. There were people who sold their labor power to others, but they weren't that many in the totality, and they could hope to have businesses and farms of their own. This was the promise of America. What has happened over 200 years is the process by which most of us became wage laborers — that is, came to work for someone else and came to work for increasingly large scale enterprises, private institutions, and so on. This is the process of proletarianization in the Marxian language; that is, the separation of people from an ability to produce what they need themselves and to exchange among themselves, to a dependence of selling their labor power in the market place, working for someone else. One part of it is the building of hierarchy specialization, segmentation, layers of supervisors, a raising of the large economic edifices in which control by people diminishes over time and control of large-scale organizations over which we have very little influence and power increases.

On the economic side, the process goes something like this: Let us say in the beginning we are producing automobiles in the back yard in a bicycle shop and our entrepreneur hires three people and together they make a car. The entrepreneur pays each of these people their wages which is enough to feed themselves, their families, perhaps put a little down-payment on a house, and so on. With what is left over afterwards, our entrepreneur says, I will use to hire two more folks to make some machines which will help us make cars better, and I can do that because they're producing enough to provide for their needs and something extra. With the machines it is now possible for these workers to produce far more cars and so to generate more surplus at the end of the process which allows the entrepreneur to hire a whole machine shop to go further.

Pretty soon this little back yard enterprise becomes General Motors, and all of us are somewhere in this hierarchy in the machine shop, or in advertising or sales. Each of us looks at this vast corporation and says, "My goodness, look at the size of this. I need a job. I hope there's a job there. I've got to go find a job somewhere. I can't start my own machine shop. I can't start my own automobile company. I must go work for someone else." In the early days, say 1920, there were a hundred automobile companies in the United States. There are now three and a quarter.

The process of concentration and centralization in the economy has been going on for 200 years and I described it not at all unreasonably in terms of how it took place. At the end of each circuit of capital accumulation, the surplus that is left over is there to be reinvested either at home or abroad in new capacity to hire new workers.

Now there are a few things that are important about this. The first is that the vast edifice of General Motors that we saw at the end of the process was historically the creation of working people over this entire process of accumulation. When a company that has been in New England for a hundred years says, "We're going to move to Taiwan, South Korea, or maybe just South Carolina," the workers are then told, "The company is not yours; you got paid fair wages, you have nothing coming. You're stuck there with your house, your community and no job; the resulting depression of your area is not our concern; we paid fair wages, we have no responsibility in an economy to take care of you, that's not our job. Go see the Government, go see the Church, go find charity organizations, do something, but it is not our responsibility."

There is a point of contention regarding the process of accumulation. The contention is around whether the social product belongs to the society (the working people who created the factories, the wealth) or whether we accept that the social surplus generated through generations of working people's efforts is to be appropriated by one small group who can then move it wherever they want. It is this question which is at the center of much of the political discussion in Europe right now. In countries like England, France, Scandinavia, Germany, to some degree, Italy — in almost all of the advanced capitalist countries of Europe, the labor movements, often with the active participation of worker priests and church groups, are involved in this great debate.

If one accepts that wealth is a social product then the way we deal with social need is very different. At a minimum, there must be policies that the company must then pay off each of the workers, must help them relocate somewhere else, must provide new jobs, must provide two years severance pay. There are different sorts of programs of different degrees, but that becomes a major social concern around an economic issue.

DUALISM IN THE ECONOMY

The second thing about this process of accumulation is what economists call dualism in the economy. The American economy today really has two parts, the private economy and the monopoly sector which is the world of the *Fortune* "Top 500," the 500 largest firms in the country, which have about two-thirds of the output of the manufacturing sector, a little more than two-thirds of the profits, and basically dominate the economy. They are less than one per cent of all the corporations in America. They're a small number, but of course they are the familiar household names, the General Electrics, the General Motors, the other Generals, who hold the commanding positions in the economy.

The other 99 and nine-tenths per cent of the corporations are small. Some of them, the second largest 500, are not really tiny, but compared to the giants they don't matter a whole lot in any real sense. They are the corner grocery store, the barber shops and the small gas stations — (if you can find one that is not a franchise of the multi-national corporations). The small, competitive firms live in a very different world.

It's called the monopoly sector because there are only a few giants in industries like steel, auto, oil, just about any breakfast cereal and tobacco. When

things become important to them which are not important to competitive firms.

For example, Exxon has probably the third best intelligence service in the world. That is, they have psychological profiles of the leaders of every nation in which they do business. This kind of information makes a difference if they're going to be nationalized or if a possessive government comes in and starts taxing them. They must be up on the internal situation in all these countries. They are aware of what Congress does. Their lobbyists are there to help out, to introduce legislation, and so on. They have power that comes from their size and that power is structural. That is, if a President of the U.S. ever started behaving in a way that the monopoly sector did not like, he would be in trouble. He would be in trouble in a number of ways. Quite obviously, the next time he ran for office there would be very little money forthcoming. There would be pressure. There would be lobbying. But more than that, it's not just a question of the structure of the economy. If you make life inhospitable to large corporations, the business climate sours. When the business climate sours, unemployment starts rising. Therefore, with the best of intentions, a politician must be very careful about how he treats large corporations. This places all politicians in a very undesirable position even if you assume politicians are the finest people in the world. But despite these structural obstacles, we need change. Discussions of reform, however, must be realistic.

The larger constraints are going to be increasingly important and we must deal with them very straight-forwardly. First, the monopoly sector in the United States is the most powerful monopoly sector in the world economy. In Germany and Japan we have other large capitalists. Multinational firms based in those countries are now able to deal with states or provinces within one nation. That is to say, if taxes are too high in Massachusetts, South Carolina will give you no taxes for 10 years, will build you a free plant, will put a highway right up to your plant, will give you a bond issue to raise money — that is, they will stand ready to do things to attract industry. Now if Massachusetts wants industry back, what will it do? When Volkswagen came to locate in the United States, they finally settled on a $70 million package with Pennsylvania. That is, Pennsylvania had to buy the location of the company.

So we have a situation where the firms are so large and so important that if you want jobs you're being told you must pay for them, a very different situation than the butcher, baker, candlestick maker serving the customers and giving them a better product.

Second, monopolies are larger and more important than most governments in the world. They have

you look at the breakfast cereal in your supermarket and you see 150 crispy crunchies and crunchy crispies and crispy crunchy crunchies, you know, that the choice really is just among three cereal companies. Only three companies produce all the cigarettes in the United States; it's the same thing if you're looking for a car. A relatively small number of firms dominate the industry. This is not to say that there is no competition. It is to say there is very little price competition. General Motors knows that if they lowered prices, they might sell more cars, but they know their competitors would also lower prices and they'd lower profits. They resisted cutting prices on cars in the worst parts of the last serious recession until very late when they finally had to do it to try and get sales up. But in the monopoly sector, prices tend to be rigid downward. That is they go up just fine, but they don't seem to go down too well. This is a situation economists call "oligopolistic interdependence," or competition among the few. That's when Ford looks at General Motors and looks at Chrysler. They understand that they're sort of in it together and it's not the same situation when one fruit stand has got to watch its prices just as another one down the line does. It's a far cry from Adam Smith's capitalism, in other words. These firms have a time horizon that goes into the infinite future and they expect to be around for a very long time and they try and control that environment to see that it's favorable to them. They are very large and certain power over governments. If you were to put the GNP of all the countries in the world as well as the sales of the companies together, General Motors would be the eighth largest country in the world, and so on down the line. They dwarf most of the countries in which they do business and increasingly have that power not only over South Korea or Nigeria but over England and increasingly here in the United States as well. When we talk about freedom of private enterprise, the question of democracy in such a context becomes complicated. Should the freedom of corporations be beyond the democratic process?

The logic of the market is such that it forces citizens in different countries to take lower taxes on corporations and higher taxes on themselves — and that in fact is what's happening. The taxes the corporations pay as a percentage of total taxes have been declining very dramatically; they're half of what they were 20 years ago. More of the taxes come from working people and increasingly from more and more regressive sources of taxation. If you tax the rich, they'll simply move to the next state that doesn't have as progressive a tax system.

The third point is the relation of monopoly to the competitive sector and the government. In the past the monopoly sector — the steel industry, auto, rubber, oil — all absorbed more labor. Now we're going the other way. The auto industry is producing more cars with fewer workers, so that's leaving those on the fringes looking for work. They will be unemployed unless some other sector in the economy is absorbing those workers. As the monopoly sector doesn't grow in terms of employment, but continues to grow in terms of output and profitability, it is in the monopoly sector that the surplus of the society is collected. However, it's throwing out lots of people. Where the sons and daughters of steel workers and auto workers might have worked in those companies, increasingly those companies don't have room for them and they must go somewhere else. They must go to some other part of those large corporations. If we divide employment into perhaps three parts: Production workers, (the blue collar workers), white collar office workers and top management, we will see that the growth has not been in blue collar jobs, but in white collar office jobs and in management, that is, jobs associated with selling the product, with designing new products, with figuring out ways of changing them to look like new products, finding new markets, and all of that. But even at that it hasn't grown enough to absorb the total labor force. Therefore, people must go to one of two places: Either to the competitive sector (and that is what's happening to a lot of people now who had aspirations of better jobs; they are driving taxicabs, are working in small firms), or to the Government.

And Government is expanding for a number of complex reasons:

The monopoly sector is not absorbing workers and the competitive sector is not absorbing them either, except in very low paid, marginal, seasonal kinds of jobs. The need for transfer payments for people who cannot keep up with inflation, have no sources of income and who would not be causing difficulties for the society as we saw in the 1960s, must be bought off somehow through some sort of program: Welfare, unemployment compensation, whatever. So one reason Government grows is because the people who do not have a place in the growing part of the economy must depend on the Government. Also, the Government is increasingly in the business of subsidizing in one way or another the accumulation process itself. The most dramatic ways are: Research and development contracts by Government, the military and highways.

In research and development I would include all of the subsidies to large corporations, tax incentives, investment tax credits, the kinds of things Government does to lower the cost to corporations so that they'll grow (i.e. reducing taxes so they'll have more money for investment and thus hopefully create jobs). That increasingly takes an awful lot of money. The reason it takes a lot of money is that these

corporations are already capital intensive. If you want to create 10 jobs in a capital intensive industry it takes a lot of capital. Since the capital you introduce is so much more efficient than the capital it replaces, you're really throwing people out of work, where you're supposedly creating jobs. You have to run faster. You have to put more into the private sector per job created. The military is the same sort of situation — very capital intensive.

"Highways" can be a shorthand for the whole complex of the post war pattern of accumulation. Why did the American economy grow after World War II? It was based not just on defense, not just Government subsidies, but the whole pattern of suburbanization. The Federal Interstate Highway Program was the largest single program in Government after defense and it went along with Government subsidies for housing, FHA, VA and so on. Suburbanization meant a construction industry boom; highways meant the automobile industry boom. When we say automobile, we mean also steel, rubber, oil and petroleum. All of the complex around highways is an incredible engine of growth in the post war period: Consumer durables like new dishwashers and new washing machines helped put General Electric in the top 500.

If you look at the large firms in the American economy, they're heavily dependent on Government policies, while they talk against socialism and Government intervention. It is often the military contractors — that whole missile crescent in the Sun Belt that grew on aircraft, on missiles and electronics — that were the beneficiaries of the Government contracts. When they talk against Government spending, you have to understand that they're talking about only one type of Government spending — the kind that helps people. They're not talking about the kind of Government spending that helps them. There have been no indications that they want their contracts cut, and that's exceedingly important if the needs of the people come first. They are on the defensive, as if we don't in fact have a system of socialism already, but it's socialism for the rich and large corporations. I think that is a point that has to be emphasized here.

So much for the dualism in the economy of the large corporations and the competitive sector, and the role of Government. Along with the monopoly sector and along with this accumulation of capital and companies getting larger and larger is the need to constantly increase sales because what any corporation must do is not just produce goods, but sell them. It is clear that the large corporations in America could produce much, much more than they produce now. Detroit could turn out twice as many cars with relatively little additional labor. We could produce much more of all of the things we need, want, don't want, the whole thing. Why isn't more produced? Because it can't be sold profitably, and the large corporations understand this and so they do not produce the maximum output. One of the things that is often said against another form of economy is that if we ever started changing the way the U.S. economy is organized, we'd go through a period of scarcity and the living standard would fall. I don't believe it for two reasons. One is the productive capacity of the United States is enormous. The problem is on the social relations side of how to get rid of it, because it is production not for use, but production for exchange, for profit in the market place. A corporation makes the decision on whether they expand output or not based on whether, if they expand output, they can sell it at a profit. If the answer is no, it does no good in the world for all the church people in America to say, "But we need these things." That is not the criteria. The incentive system for a large corporation is the bottom line. It is *profit*. Unless you're willing to face and discuss that, it is very difficult to conceive of change, and I think that's exceedingly important.

ACCUMULATION PHENOMENA

We understand now that products are designed to go wrong, that if the parts are shoddy, they're made to be shoddy. Millions of dollars are spent every year to be sure that things run out on time. They break down according to schedule.

If in fact you made a car that ran for 10 years, as indeed we could, who would buy a new car next year? The styles change, the package changes, clothing changes. Clothing used to be consumer durables. You know — you bought a suit and you wore it for 20 years. In addition to waste, another phenomena of accumulation is the effect it has on ecology. The core of the whole ecological question is very much rooted in the nature of the accumulation process. If goods were made to last, you would not have the incredible waste. If the sales effort did not dominate corporations you would not have this vast army of sales people getting on those planes in every airport in the country to fly out in the morning and fly back at night, using an incredible amount of energy. All of that fuel cost! If you were to start calculating all of the expenditures that basically don't increase welfare, but are necessary to keep the system going as opposed to serving the needs of people, you see an incredible amount of waste, much of it unnecessary.

The other thing that is going on besides the wastefulness of the sales effort is the increasing multinationalization of production and this gets us closer to the present in some very important ways. The multinational corporation creates dislocation everywhere because the multinational corporations are larger than most nations and all nations must respect them in the ways I've described. Now I want to be a bit more specific about this process of multinationalization and describe some of the things that are happening.

One of the things is technically called *multiple sourcing*. I was recently visiting with some labor folks in the Mid-West and met a woman who works in an Essex Wiring Plant. You probably don't know about this plant unless you follow labor struggles closely.

Essex is part of a multinational conglomerate called United Technologies which has subsidiaries all over the world. The Mid-West Plant (which is a UAW Plant) employs women, mostly from 45 to 55, who don't want to go on welfare. There are no other jobs in this area, so they work for very low wages. This particular plant went on strike for over a year and lost. The women from Essex told me that eight other plants in other parts of the world produced the same thing they did (including one in Ireland). When they went on strike, the company said, "Well, that's all right. This is our offer. This is what it will be a year from now when you go back to work. We have other ways of getting this thing and if you want to keep at this we'll just close the plant totally." The company was able to say this to each of the other plants. This is called multiple sourcing. What companies have found out is that producing everything in one huge factory is a bad deal for them because when working conditions are bad, when company profits

are high and wages are not being improved, and when workers feel safety conditions are not being looked after, they go on strike. If a company can move into multiple sourcing across many nations, it is awfully hard for workers to get together and strike.

The "fighting grannies," as the Union organization was called, struck against the company as well as against the UAW which was their organizational union and has embarked on a policy of trying to organize themselves with the other affiliates to try to get to a position where they can take on Essex and United Technologies. This is very encouraging and very exciting. The strike itself was incredible because it got the support of local community people and local church people who understood that the striking workers were their neighbors who were being oppressed and exploited by this huge conglomerate, who were playing one group of workers against another and profiting at their expense. This is the kind of connections that people are beginning to make. These are just ordinary people in a rural part of Ohio, yet they became the most beautiful militant class-conscious people after the strike. They've been having parties to commemorate the strike in the plant as a way of reminding the workers that it was only the first and now they're fighting with the UAW to start making connections with the other workers in other places. I think that the multinational corporations must be fought that way.

It is exceedingly important that we identify with these movements, that we consider their struggle our struggle because the multinational corporations are the clear and present danger in the world today to any kind of notion of social justice and the kind of egalitarian society we want.

ALIENATION

I want to introduce the concept of alienation, but perhaps in a somewhat different context than we're used to hearing it, by talking about the Marxian theory of alienation.

The Marxian theory of alienation seeks to explain how individuals in capitalist society have lost their understanding and control of the world around them and have in the process been stunted and perverted into something less than being fully human. For Marx the source of all alienation lies in the social relations of work. Alienation means that individuals no longer have an immediate and intimate relationship to the environment. They have been specialized and sorted, made into what Marx calls, "the most wretched of commodities," divorced from the products they produce, split into mental and manual workers, divided into dominant and subordinate classes, thrown into selfish competition with one another. The notion of alienation is the core

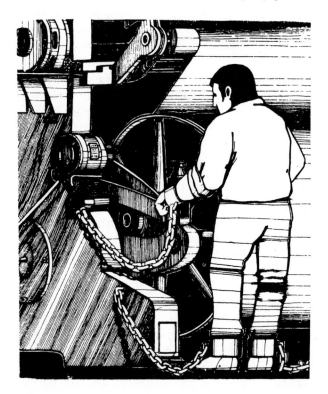

notion for Marx because it defines so much of the problem of the society.

There are three aspects of the concept I want to talk about. Before I do that, however, let me note that alienation does not originate in a psychological state but in an economic place. The relation between the psychological and the economic is very important for us to understand so that we do not do what some economists do and just deal with the economic, nor what many church people do, and merely speak about the psychological and the spiritual dimension of alienation.

There are three parts to this relation. The first, and the most basic, is the class relationship between capital and labor. It is a relationship that we can term the "dirty secret", which guides and determines the shape of our society — who we are and how we are respected or not respected by others. The capital-labor relationship is a relationship of conflict. I want to discuss it in terms of the notion of full employment which is something we are all for. Why would anybody be against full employment? Isn't full employment something everyone in the society wants, something everyone needs? The answer is *no*.

Picture if you will a period of full employment. Use your imaginations now and think back to World War I or World War II or the Korean War or the Vietnamese War for us younger folks. I was teaching at the University of Connecticut at the height of the Vietnam War. From Hartford, which was our nearest big town, every 15 minutes on the radio there would be ads for machinists, for anybody, to come work in the huge aircraft factory of Pratt and Whitney in Hartford. They would come to your home; they would send their wagon around to your neighborhood at night; the recruiting office at the plant was open on weekends; they told you how great it was to work there. It was really pretty good in terms of competing jobs.

I wasn't the only one listening to that radio program. Every worker and every employer in the Hartford area knew the given labor scarcity. Employers who had treated their workers badly, who had ignored safety conditions, who had paid low wages, or who had forced every ounce of energy out of their workers, knew that those conditions had better improve a little bit because their workers were voting with their feet. They weren't even bothering to talk about it. When there's full employment, there's a choice of jobs. When there is a choice of jobs, the power relation between worker and capitalist changes dramatically. Things that were thought unheard of in periods of high unemployment were of course granted in full employment. The employer knew that the worker could get another job. Unions gained courage in that knowledge and made

demands; unorganized workers are respected to a degree that is never the case in periods of high unemployment.

In periods of high unemployment, on the other hand, we're glad for the job we have if we're employed. We know that there are a lot of people who would take it. If we don't like it, it's much harder to organize. It's much harder to pull workers together. Our working conditions deteriorate when people are fired or retire or move and are not replaced. For example, I have to teach many more courses now, with many more students. My life has changed very dramatically because of the cutbacks in the University. In factories, the accident rate increases dramatically as unemployment goes up.

This does not mean that in periods of unemployment, the workers don't fight back. They do. Strikes increase. Militant actions increase. But they are conditioned by the unemployment rate, as a significant level of unemployment always is a tool of employers against workers, and it is for that reason that full employment is not the goal of employers or politicians who are strongly beholden to employers. On the whole what's important to understand is this notion of capital and labor being antagonistically related. It is in the interest of the employer to see that the employee works harder and produces more, because the more that's produced, the more profit there is.

Further, and this we may have disagreements on, it is difficult to be a good employer in a Christian sense. Some of us know of good employers. But it is exceedingly difficult because a good employer faces competition from a bad employer. The bad employer produces the product and it sells for a penny less. The consumer goes to the shelf, sees the difference, buys the cheaper one. The employers who can force more out of their workers can reduce that price just a little bit and can profit from it. So it is difficult for capitalists even with a Christian background to be good, since they are caught in a structural situation. What I'm trying to stress is the structural role of antagonism between capital and labor which is forced on both groups. Workers do not want to come home at the end of the day so exhausted all they can do is sit with a can of beer and watch television. They're just too worn out to do anything else. They have been dehumanized by an employer who must force every ounce of effort out of them or a competitor will. It is the pressure of the capital-labor relationship. It is a contradictory relationship, an antagonistic relationship and that's all part of the system.

The second form of alienation is between worker and worker. Why between worker and worker? Because as long as there is five or 10 per cent unemployment, you must work harder or you will be part of that five or 10 per cent. The job is structured on promotion ladders, but if you are not working harder than someone else you don't get promoted. There are other workers who want your promotion and you are competing against them. The work situation is structured so that workers compete with each other. Moreover, the employed compete not only with each other but also with the unemployed, who want your job.

Work is structured to maximize that competition. For example, envision a factory in which everyone works together and gets paid the same amount of money. In fact we have some experiments of this sort. My favorite case study is of a dog food factory. The general idea was that the workers could do whatever they wanted as long as the dog food gets produced at the end. The production was structured so that there were about twelve jobs and workers rotated among the jobs. One got paid more money if one could do different jobs. Pretty soon workers understood all the jobs from unloading the stuff at one end to running the stuff through the mixer and processor to doing the chemical analysis to packaging and loading it up. There was only one problem with this. The problem was not that the production went down; no, production went up. It was not that the workers weren't happy; no, they liked it. It was that management was left with nothing to do. Management is to make workers work. A foreman stood around watching all the jobs, but he didn't have to tell anybody to get back to work. Workers understood that if they finished early, they had the time off.

One other problem was that workers started doing the accounting and figured out how much profit the company was making from each of them. Before, they had looked at this vast corporation where they were glad they had a job and they did their thing.

This is the process that has gone on, especially in many European countries, around workers' control, self-management and a movement to take away from capital the prerogatives of controlling the work process by refusing to obey management. Workers have instituted parallel structures where shop stewards make the decisions. If management doesn't like it, the workers just shut down production. Can they do that? Only if the workers in the other plants of the company understand and respect what they are doing. It is that kind of power and understanding that unites workers and keeps them from fighting against each other.

The typical job of course isn't structured in that way. Anybody who's worked in any organization knows you come in at the bottom with the worst job. If you behave, you move up. However, anyone who's ever worked in a factory knows there's a base-ment, there's a foundry, there's a terrible hot place with unpleasant work from which Third World workers don't get promoted. They're not part of the job ladder, or their job ladder is very limited. On the other hand, white males with college degrees wear suits and stay in air-conditioned offices. Women only hold certain jobs. White women with college degrees have expensive clothes so they can be secretaries. That segmentation and stratification is crucial to keeping the system going. Everyone has a little bit of privilege, is a little bit better off than someone else in the structure. So that after you've invested 10 years in seniority, your job is a little easier with someone else doing the hard work. You don't give thought to the question of how much better it could be for every worker, including those who are now relatively privileged if all of the workers organized. So the segmentation, the stratification, the resulting hatred between groups that keeps the structure going oppresses everyone in that structure. It is not to say everyone is exploited to the same degree or that everyone is oppressed in the same way. It is the differential of oppression that is functional to the system.

Worker-worker competition, stratification, racism and sexism, all of these things function for the system, and that's the second element of alienation I've just discussed. We are alienated from our fellow workers, from people who are our brothers and sisters, and that alienation is rooted in the organization of work.

The third form of alienation comes from the competition between capitalists themselves. Capitalists unite when there's a threat against them from the working class but most of the time they're faced with competition from other capitalists. This alienated relationship is the inability, structurally, to change the nature of production because capitalist *must* compete with capitalist. They produce primarily for exchange, not for use or in terms of need.

Before there was capitalism, people produced what they needed and if they produced more than they actually needed they exchanged with somebody else for something they wanted. There was exchange. But production was basically for use. Now corporations don't care what they produce. They'll produce anything — bombs, pesticides, or plastic things. The question is, "Does it make money?" It is production for exchange, not for use, which is the last part of this complex notion of alienation. Individuals are estranged from fellow workers, estranged from the product they produce since many people don't even know what it is they produce. They're part of this huge edifice; they don't care, or they care but don't like it. They are alienated from the work process itself. Routine operation done over and over again is not a satisfying life. All the forms of alienation come from the basic production for profit rather than for use and this is the core of capitalism. When we talk about the "system" we have to be aware of all of the dimensions.

A NEW MODEL

Now I want to talk about models of accumulation. I talked about the post war period in the United States as being premised on the automobile, highways, military, energy-intensive and consumer durables. To keep this pattern of accumulation going is very expensive. Energy costs have risen very dramatically. Resource use has escalated, as more people want to have a higher standard of living. We're beginning to run out of raw materials, and so we're told, we can't have as much. We've got to "reduce expectations." We've got to have more "realistic standards". But we do it in a very funny way. We do it by propping up the largest giant corporations in the country. We are told that the only way we can have work is if these huge corpora-

tions have high profits. That is the model of accumulation people suggest for us. And they're saying, "it's true, you have less and less, but it could be worse," and "it's the only kind of system there can be." Keep feeding these dinosaurs and maybe there'll be some crumbs.

We need three things for a different model of accumulation. The first is that we need to fully understand the system we live in and to have a clear critique of what's wrong with that system.

Second, we must have faith and the belief that through our actions, the actions of ordinary people working together, the system can be changed; and third, we must have a vision of an alternative, a way of living, a way of relating to each other that is meaningful to us and that is possible for us; and we must make real our visions and our dreams in ways that others can understand, relate to and build on. All three are necessary. It is not enough to understand that it's a rotten system; that can lead to cynicism and apathy. It's not enough to know that you can change and destroy; you must have a vision of an alternative.

There is an alternative pattern of accumulation which I believe is realistic!

If the problem now is that we use too much of non-replenishable resources, that the environment is being destroyed, or being fouled beyond endurance, that we don't have energy and all the other resources, then we need a pattern of accumulation that is, first, labor intensive, not capital intensive. If you've been walking around New York and have seen both the need we have there and the human resources that are not being utilized, then the pattern of accumulation must be one that uses people to rebuild our environment and our living space, so that the kind of things that we have always been for — day care centers, community run enterprises, rebuilding of our cities, making it possible for people to stay on their farms — all of the policies which they say are Utopian and unrealistic are not only very realistic, but very necessary.

These policies speak of the very needs of our times: Jobs for people who need jobs, conservation of resources and energy, building and rebuilding in place of destruction. All of these things are really the only realistic policy because the alternative is too costly, we can't afford it. To carry out their policies, we are squeezed even more. What I would propose, is reversing that. They can afford to be squeezed far more. We can't continue with the present policies of maintaining the large corporations. I would say tomorrow let the structures of the large corporations fall. It is with the people in those structures who must have alternatives, and *there are alternatives*. But we do not need to hold up the dinosaurs for the little bit of good that they end up doing us. The alternative pattern of accumulation must be one that speaks to human needs, because we have both a commitment and a need as individuals in a society. As an economist, I say this is the necessary pattern of accumulation for a truly human society.   ■

Historical Materialism

by Frank Cunningham

With the exception of the idle rich, people must work to stay alive. In this way humans are like other animals. However, humans differ from other animals in the *way* they work and in the *effects* they have on nature and on themselves in the process. Lacking the sharp claws, tough hides or other natural equipment that make the survival of other species possible, humans use their hands and their brains to make *tools* and they work *socially*, by dividing up the jobs that need to be done. Some other animals use simple tools (for instance, some birds use sticks to dig bugs

Frank Cunningham is an associate professor of philosophy at the University of Toronto. This abridged article is excerpted from his book, *Understanding Marxism*, Chapter 4. Reprinted with permission of Progress Books, 71 Bathurst St., Toronto, Ontario, Canada. Copyright © 1977 by Progress Books.

out of tree bark), and there are animals that have a simple division of labor as when male lions drive prey into areas where female lions are lying in wait for them. But no animals other than humans can produce even such a simple tool as a bow and arrow, let alone a steamship or a modern factory. Even early societies contained a greater division of labor than is found among other animals — some hunted while others planted, wove, made pots, and so on. Of course there is nothing at all in the world of other animals to compare with the highly complex division of labor of modern societies.

The effect of this division of labor and use of tools has been that humans not only survived but produced more than was necessary for one generation to stay alive. Hence, each generation of humans has left behind it more than it started with. Using this surplus, people could be freed to do different kinds of

labor, to acquire different skills and to develop new tools, so the division of labor and technological development became more and more complex. The production of a surplus has had another effect as well. It has made it possible for some people not to work at all, but to live off the labor of those who do work.

These facts about the nature of human work are central to the Marxist theory of history — "historical materialism." It is a general scientific theory that guides Marxists in their efforts to understand the past and to change the present. Among other things, this theory explains how capitalism came into existence in the first place, and why it is now being replaced by socialism.

To study anything scientifically it is necessary to *classify* the subject matter and to *explain* what goes on in that subject matter by discovering laws of its behavior. Neither classifications nor laws are easy to find. They do not "jump out" of a subject matter, so to speak, and reveal themselves to a scientist, but have to be discovered by much careful investigation. For instance, it took the science of chemistry well over a century to discover the classification of chemical elements and the laws of chemical combination that we learn in high-school chemistry classes today. In a similar way, Marx and Engels had to study the process of human history carefully and learn from both the correct insights and the mistakes of previous thinkers — as well as examining the practical struggles of their own times — before they could formulate the basic tenets of historical materialism. They took as their starting place the social use of tools by humans.

MODE OF PRODUCTION

The basic Marxist category within human societies is the "mode of production." This category is made up to two things: The "forces of production" and the "relations of production." The forces of production include such things as tools and machines, systems of transport, factory buildings and warehouses, land, sources of energy and raw materials — in short, the "means of production." Of course the forces of production also include the working people themselves who use these means of production to transform nature into products suitable for human use. In early society the means of production were simple — hammers, crude plows and so on. In more complex societies they include sophisticated things like modern factories or power plants.

The "relations of production" refer most importantly to the division in a society between those who own its means of production and those who do not own any means of production and are therefore obliged to work for those who do, to stay alive. This is the *class* division between owners and workers.

An "economic class" is a group who share a common relation to the means of production. The "ruling class" owns the key means of production in a society. Owning these means, they are able to compel others to work for them and to take the fruits of this work for themselves. The capitalist class, also called the "bourgeoisie," includes those who privately own and control the major means of production in an economy based on mass producing commodities. Private owners of large means of distribution and of the banks and other major financial institutions are also considered parts of the capitalist class by most Marxists. These three sectors of the capitalist class closely interact and there is much overlap in their membership. An earlier ruling class was made up of feudal lords, who owned farmland (either directly or as agents of a king) that was worked by "serfs." Still earlier there were "slaveholders" who, among other things, owned other people.

The "working class" or "proletariat" is made up of those people who do not own any means of production but must work for people who do. Sometimes Marxists use "proletariat" to mean only the industrial working class, or those whose work is most directly related to the production of surplus value, as that term is defined. Factory workers, miners, transport

"A mixed economy, Parsons, means that you do the work and we get the profits!"

and construction workers and others engaged in large-scale production and distribution fall into this category. Their work makes them the most highly-disciplined segment of the working class with the most experience in organizing against the effects of capitalism. Members of the industrial working class tend to form the core of revolutionary political parties in industrialized societies.

In addition to the industrial working class, there are service workers, clerical workers and many others. Their labor is less directly related to the creation of surplus value; however, as capitalism develops they are increasingly forced into regimented work similar to that of the industrial working class. Changes in technology have also affected industrial work by demanding more skills of industrial workers and by requiring closer coordination between work in factories and work outside them. Because of these changes, the industrial working class has grown and diversified its modes of work and has been able to find more and more allies among other segments of the working class.

Under capitalism, not everyone is either a member of the capitalist class or of the proletariat. Marx and Engles noted several other groups and classes. There are those people who privately own a small means of production or distribution which they must work themselves or with the help of their families or a few employees in order to make a profit. These members of the "petty-bourgeoisie" include people who own small businesses, shopkeepers and family farmers who own their own farms. There are also people sometimes called members of the "middle class," like lawyers, doctors, professional engineers and people who work in corporations as middle management. Some of these people are self-employed, but even when they work for salaries, their work is not as highly organized as that of the working class and they usually make more money. Also, they are often hired to supervise other employees and increase productivity.

Some people in the petty-bourgeoisie and from the middle class realize that it is in their interests to line up with the working class against capitalists. In fact, some have no choice, since the economic squeeze created by the domination of a few large monopoly capitalist interests hurts them as well as the working class and forces some of them into the working class. Others from these groups throw in their lot with the capitalists, as do some of the chronically unemployed and down and out (the "lumpen-proletariat"). Farmers often, but not always, line up with city workers against capitalism.

Historical materialists do not present their categories as a complete classification of absolutely everything that can be found in human society. They do present their classifications as representing groups and relationships which actually exist in society and which are the most important for understanding and changing things. As with the classifications of any scientific theory, there are borderline cases where it is not clear which class a person fits into, but the general meanings of Marxist classifications are clear enough. These meanings must be kept in mind to avoid confusion. Owning a house or a car does not make someone a capitalist. For this you need to own something like a factory and employ people to create surplus value for you. A capitalist who chooses to work in his own factory or bank, as some do in a management capacity, does not therefore become a worker. He does not have to work unless he wants to, and his economically central role is as an owner and employer.

Those, then, are the components of society's mode of production: The mode of production is often called the "economic base" of society by historical materialists. Societies also include political institutions — the government and the courts, with systems of law and agencies like the army and the police to enforce them. And, in every society there are ideas: Philosophical ideas, morality, religion, cultural and scientific views. Historical materialists call all these institutions and ideas the "superstructure" of society. Political institutions are the "political" or "legal-political" part of the superstructure, while the main systems of ideas are referred to as its "ideological superstructure." (Sometimes the word "ideology" is more narrowly used by Marxists to describe just some of the leading ideas of a society, namely those unscientific ideas which only serve to rationalize oppressive rule.)

LAWS OF HISTORICAL MATERIALISM

Marxist social scientists have discovered many laws of social development, some more general than others. Here I will summarize two of the most general laws of historical materialism. First, by and large, a society's superstructure is determined by its economic base. Specifically, in a class-divided society the type of existing political system is determined by the needs of that society's ruling class, and the dominant ideas of the society are for the most part the ideas of its ruling class.

This finding is disputed by practically all anti-Marxist social scientists, and Marxism is denounced as crude and simplistic for advancing it, but people must work to stay alive, and it would be most strange if the tools used and the social relations guiding this work did not shape the rest of society. Surely it is no accident that complex governmental forms and scientific theories like those of modern physics did not appear in ancient times. As each and every 17th and 18th Century European society began to change its methods of production to ones with capitalist relations of production, similar changes followed in the country's type of government. Parliamentary governments were formed (which, as we will see, are best suited to capitalist interests), and the dominant philosophical ideas changed from medieval religious views to ones favoring scientific invention and economic competition.

The other main law of historical materialism is that major changes within a society's mode of production are caused by conflicts between its forces and relations of production. In very early societies, where hunters and gatherers used simple tools, there were no class divisions. This was not because people in these societies, called "primitive communism" by Marx and Engels, were believers in socialist theory, but simply because there was very little division of labor and the economy was not sophisticated enough for anyone to privately hoard a surplus. The forces of production in early societies were mainly human hands and brains aided by very simple tools. The relations of production were equally simple — little division of labor and no ruling class.

There are ongoing debates among Marxist anthropologists over the nature of these hunting and gathering classless societies and how they changed into class-divided ones. Following the most advanced anthropological thinking of their time, Marx and Engels seemed to have held that there were no ruling classes because life was too hard, so there was no surplus above what was needed to keep the members of a tribe alive for anyone to exploit. However, hunting and gathering work, primitive as it was, eventually led to several changes in society that undermined the early communistic nature of this mode of work itself. Contact between tribes created trade. It led to war and the taking of captives as slaves. Standing armies came into existence. Agriculture replaced hunting, and for the first time, some people found themselves not hunting, farming or doing any kind of physical labor. They found themselves also in a position to personally control the new means of production and to take as their own the surplus created by the rest of the tribe. New relations of production appeared and humanity entered the period of history in which societies are torn by class division between rulers and ruled.

More recent work, by both Marxists and non-Marxist anthropologists, suggests that in most, if not all places, early hunters and gatherers did not experience want. Compared to the peasants who succeeded them, they worked fewer hours and consumed a more adequate and varied diet. What these people did lack was a technology of food preservation, that is, the ability to accumulate a surplus which would free some from the daily necessity to hunt and gather. This possibility emerged only with agriculture, when some people freed from productive labor, took personal control of agricultural land.

Whatever the various origins of class-divided society might have been, Marx and Engels noted that from the point where classes emerged history progressed differently in different parts of the world. Areas of Asia developed in one way, of Europe in another, depending on raw materials available, geography and the specific means of production that took hold. In the history of Europe, egalitarian communities gave way to large land-and-slave-holding empires. These in turn were replaced by feudalism, which was replaced by capitalism.

In each transformation the pattern was the same. Forces of production that at one time worked in relative harmony with certain relations of production outgrew them and these relations of production became fetters on developing forces. At the same time, new relations of production came into being and encouraged new productive forces. For instance, under feudalism the means of production included farm implements, crude mining and irrigational tools and relatively simple devices to aid manufacture and navigation. Ruling class feudal lords took a major portion of what was produced by farming serfs. However, with increased trade and manufacture, new classes of manufacturers and merchants emerged to develop new and profitable means of production. Geared to agriculture and simple trade, the old relations of production began to retard the development of trade and large-scale manufacture. Feudal relations gave way to new relations in which capitalists became the ruling class. They employed city workers who had left the farms (forming an industrial proletariat) and developed the tremendous potential of new technology. These changes in the relations of production were accompanied by political developments in which bourgeois revolutions (all of them involving violence) replaced feudal states with capitalist-dominated ones.

World capitalism now faces a situation where the productive forces that it developed have outgrown capitalist relations of production. Industrialized production has become too massive and interdependent to be run by individual competitive capitalists who are driven by the profit motive. The effects of technological changes are too long-term and too important to be guided by such short-term individual desires. The contradiction between social labor and private ownership is formidable. One effect of this contradiction is the mess all capitalist economies are in. Food in one part of the world is destroyed, while in other parts of the world (or even in the same country) people starve. There is chronic unemployment.

Inflation continues. The gap between rich and poor widens. And social revolution occurs as working people organize to take political power and institute social ownership of the means of production.

The pattern of changing relations of production is as before, but with an important difference. For the first time it is working people themselves who are taking control of the means of production, not a small group of people who do not themselves work.

what happens in the superstructure is caused by what happens in the economic base, there are also causes that work the other way. One example is the scientific discoveries that lead to the invention of new tools or means of production.

In saying that the economic base is central for social change, Marxists mean that the *overall pattern* of historical change can only be understood and predicted by looking at the changing way people

A socialist transformation is one in which the majority of the people, those who do the actual work, become the ruling class. In this respect socialism marks a major turning point in history. It begins an era in which the mighty tools that humans have created can finally be used in a planned and rational way for the benefit of humanity as a whole.

EVERYTHING TO ECONOMICS?

Marx and Engels never held that absolutely everything that happens in history is caused by economic factors. On the contrary, Marxists maintain that non-economic factors have important effects on a society's economy. To put this in historical-materialist terms, Marxists maintain that while

work, not by looking just at the governmental forms or theories people have. Major changes in the superstructure can be made if there is a major change in the economic base, but not the other way around. Therefore, Marxists maintain that political revolutions require certain economic bases and cannot be artificially imposed. Although the superstructure can affect the base, it cannot do so unless the base is itself developed sufficiently to be affected. For instance, while scientific discoveries revolutionized industry in the 18th Century, those same discoveries would not have had the same effect in earlier societies. In fact, the steam engine was discovered in ancient Greece, but since the forces and relations of production were too underdeveloped to convert to industrialization, it was just used as a toy by the rich.

"The secret of my success, Henry, lies in the very sound advice my father once gave me. 'Son,' he said, 'Here's a million dollars. Don't lose it'."

Another common criticism of historical materialism is that it does not take into account how people think of themselves. Anti-Marxist sociologists regularly do opinion surveys to show that while Marxists might consider all the factory workers in a country members of the proletariat, some of these workers think of themselves as middle class or maybe some even as upper class. This approach of bourgeois theorists, called "subjectivism," suggests that people are just what they think they are.

The subjective criticism of Marxism would have some weight if people *never* came to see themselves as being accurately described by the Marxist classifications. However, while some people can maintain illusions about their place in society, very few can maintain them for long. I imagine that in a small plant a factory worker might help to make some minor management decisions and even feel chummy with the boss, thus gaining the illusion of being part of management. But this attitude is hard to maintain when he is fired by his "chum" or when the boss sells the business and retires to Florida leaving his fellow "manager" to join the ranks of the unemployed.

Subjectivists also criticize Marxists for not being "humanistic." They claim that by classifying people in economic terms, Marxists cease to be concerned with people's personal, human qualities — their hopes and fears, their values and beliefs. If Marxists weren't concerned about these things, they would not work so hard to create a world where people's hopes can be realized and inhuman values like racism are not bred. But to build such a world we must figure out how the present one works, and for this we need the scientific categories that best explain it.

Thinking of people in terms of their mode of work is completely compatible with thinking of them in truly human terms. Work is the transformation of nature into humanly useful things. Human work shapes and in turn is shaped by human values and beliefs. If work becomes debasing, cold and inhuman, it is not because there is something wrong with the human transformation of nature. The problem lies with the capitalist rule, where people do not work for themselves but for the private profit of those who care little about the quality of work or its effects on humans, other species and nature. Wanting to understand how this takes place in order to change it is a deeply humanistic goal.

Because anti-Marxist theorists believe it is impossible to give any general explanations of what happens in history, they have devoted much energy to trying to show that historical materialism cannot be correct. Despite the cleverness of many of their arguments, I do not believe that purely abstract arguments can settle this question. It is necessary to look at actual historical facts to decide whether they are best explained by historical materialism, or by some other theory, or whether they are explained by no theory at all. ∎

Contribution to Our Museum

by Marge Piercy

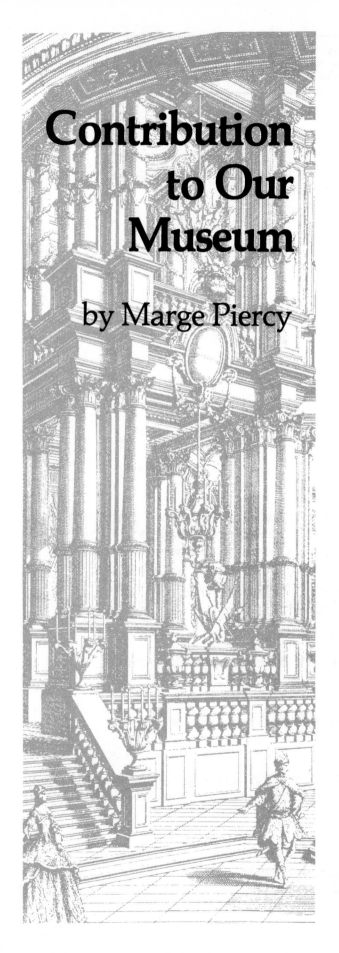

I cannot worship ancestors.
All the tall ruffled ghosts
kept servants who pressed those linen shirts,
who murmur still in the carved and fitted stone
the life that was stolen from them.

In each cut diamond is hardened the anguish
carbonized of choking miners.
Each ruby bleeds the buried cries
of women who bloated with hunger after they
        harvested.
Each opal secretes the milky grief
of babies bombed sedately by computer
or spitted on bayonets in the Indian wars.

The gentry dance at the Diamond Ball at the Plaza
charitably, on behalf of third world education.
In the gutter the dead leaves scuttle,
the hungry rustle on the wind blowing
up from Bolivia, which the oil men own.

Always in the tidy fiefdoms of history taught
Louis on the guillotine is weighed in chapters
while fifty thousand peasants who starved
are penned in a textual note.
My folks were serfs, miners, factory women.
Their bent shoulders never bore the brocades in
        those cases.
They did not embroider the gossip at Versailles.
They were not invited to hunt with the czarina.

How can I love Mount Vernon
with its green alleys and its river perspective
and its slave quarters?
When the ghosts of Susan B. Anthony and
        Mother Jones,
of Harriet Tubman and Tecumseh and
        August Spies
dance on our small smokes as we picnic on the
        lawn,
we will preserve the slave quarters tenderly
because there are no more ghettos, no wage-slaves
and no soft domestic slavery bounded by rape.

The past leads to us if we force it to.
Otherwise it contains us
in its asylum with no gates.
We make history or it
makes us.

Group Exercise

Divide your group into smaller groups of no more than five people each. Air any questions of interpretation related to the Cunningham and Tabb articles, making sure members of the group have grasped the major concepts. Below is a listing of some of them:

- mode of production
- means of production
- relations of production
- working class or proletariat
- bourgeoisie
- petty-bourgeoisie
- surplus value
- superstructure
- laws of historical materialism
- process of concentration and centralization
- monopoly sector of the economy
- competitive sector of the economy
- multiple sourcing
- alienation

For the remainder of this session, each group participant will share his/her family history, focusing on economic and class backgrounds. In telling your story start as far back as you have knowledge and proceed to the present. A facilitator should divide up the time into even segments, so that each person has a chance to speak. The following questions, as well as Sheila Collins' article, can serve as a guide.

1 What did your great-grandparents, grandparents, mother/father do for a living?

2 How did all of these people feel about their vocation/work? How did others perceive them?

3 What factors motivated or conditioned their particular vocation? If certain economic circumstances were different, would they have chosen differently?

4 What factors caused them to make major changes in their lives (such as deciding to get married, to have children, to move from one place or job to another, to go to school, *etc*.)?

5 Try to relate these changes to shifts that were occurring in the larger economy at the time, as described by Cunningham and Tabb.

6 How do you think your family's economic/class background has affected you? For example, how has it affected your self-image, your job expectations, your feelings about your parents, your perceptions of others?

7 What religious themes stand out in the telling of your story? How was/is your religious practice influenced by your class background and present location?

Use the last half hour of your time together for group discussion. Examine the following additional questions:

8 Did you learn anything new about yourself or others through this kind of discussion?

9 Why do you think the churches have avoided dealing with questions of class and economics?

10 What is the significance of Marge Piercy's line: "We make history, or it makes us."

SESSION 3

Confronting
Capitalism

A most dramatic moment of stage and screen came in a recent production of *The Miracle Worker*, when a blind-and-mute child named Helen Keller was desperately trying to be reached by her teacher, Annie Sullivan. Annie would constantly and repetitively spell the name of objects into Helen's hand while the child touched them so Helen might be given tools that would unlock the mysterious world around her through some *system*.

"It has a name, Helen: T-r-e-e. Tree. . . . She has a name: M-o-t-h-e-r. . . ." Then after long, agonizing efforts, the climax, when somehow Helen realized that the "stuff" coming out of the pump was "w-a-t-e-r." And a whole new world opened up for the child, heretofore locked in darkness.

Our study proceeds somewhat like that. In previous sessions, we have been investigating our lives as individuals, trying to share and name some of the pain we feel in our work situations. Subsequently, we traced our family histories through the world of work to get a better picture of our heritage. We also saw that the way people act and think is largely determined by the way they make their living and the way their work is organized. And we were presented some tools for analysis that we might demystify the seemingly complicated situation of the workplace.

In this session, we move on to name and examine the economic foundation of our society — the system of capitalism. At one time, many called this system *free enterprise*, in which anyone who worked hard could make it to the top. Moreover, it was believed that excesses could be corrected and, with careful planning and a better distribution of goods, the United States and other Western capitalist countries could "feed the world" and bring about "development."

By now inflation and unemployment alone have led most to disbelief. This chapter is dedicated to examining some of the other myths attached to the thinking that the capitalist system is still the best system in or for the world. For example, is economic progress simply a matter of a more equitable distribution of wealth — a better "delivery system" from the rich nations to the poor — or should we be asking deeper questions about ownership of production?

In this session, we turn to a more analytical examination of the way our economy is organized, the driving motivation of private profit and its consequences upon the peoples of the world. In our deliberations, words and their use become extremely important. Rather than speak of the *rich* and the *poor*, we try to analyze the plight of *working people*. In the process, we bump our heads against other words: Exploiter and exploited, oppressor and oppressed — terms which are charged with political and moral responsibility.

Most of us are committed to a type of economic democracy that would guarantee everyone an equal voice in the control of the productive assets to assure a fully human life. But today, systemic forces are operating in our society which advocate the opposite — an international trade and monetary system controlled by a privileged class.

While the *name* capitalism did not emerge until later, the *process* began in the 17th Century with European penetration of Latin America, Africa and Asia, and the forced orientation of the economy and agriculture of these regions to serve the purposes and whims of industrializing countries. Indigenous economic patterns were truncated or destroyed, and agriculture for internal consumption was turned to cash cropping for export. The African slave trade and comparable forms of forced labor in Latin America disrupted family life and social structures. The result was genocide for entire populations. Colonialism forced people to work as unskilled labor at starvation wages.

In this century, global corporations have introduced technologies designed to enhance private consumption, not to solve social problems.

As far back as 1848 in the *Communist Manifesto*, Marx and Engels pointed out that capitalism is a restlessly expanding system which "cannot exist without constantly revolutionizing the instruments of production, and thereby the relations of production, and with them the whole relations of society." Moreover, "the need of a constantly expanding market for its products chases the bourgeoisie over the whole surface of the globe." They noted that this system was pre-eminently a market, or commodity producing economy, which "has left no other nexus between man and man than naked self-interest, than callous cash payment."

Whether we agree with the Marxist analysis and the chances of capitalism's survival or not, since more than one-third of the world's population is now living under socialism, it is well to explore what socialists believe about our system. The companion reading piece in this session is by a contemporary, Frank Cunningham, who presents a classic Marxist analysis of capitalism in simple terms. This type of analysis has proven vital to many Christians in Europe and Latin America who have been in dialogue and working relationships with Marxists for social change.

Looked at from the point of view of Christian missionaries, such as the following reading by Toland *et al*, or from the point of view of a Marxist scholar, our economic system has a name: "C-a-p-i-t-a-l-i-s-m." After previous chapters and this present examination, we would hope to have a better grasp of what the consequences of capitalism are, not only upon our own lives, but also upon the lives of our brothers and sisters throughout the world. ■

The Myths of Capitalism

The Rich Get Richer And The Poor Get...

World justice and peace are top priorities on the churches agendum.

As church people, however, it would be well to recognize some of the biases we might bring to our considerations of justice and peace. For example, we are often more comfortable with church statements and theologies of development which exhort us to be concerned about the poor than with doing the homework needed to grasp the economic, political and historical facts that underlie particular injustices.

We also tend to deal with problems only at the

Written by Lawrence McCulloch, Thomas Fenton and Gene Toland for the Maryknoll Education Project for Justice and Peace in 1972 and updated by Elaine Fuller in 1979. Reprinted by permission of the authors.

individual, person-to-person level. Especially today when so much emphasis is put on the personal and the psychological, we tend to neglect the impact of institutions and systems on people. We often ignore the fact that certain systems, e.g. slavery, are in themselves unjust and therefore must be changed if we are to have any hope for justice and peace.

A third bias we can have as church people is to misread Christ's command to "love our enemies," so that our anger and impatience at injustice are neutralized. There was no paralysis in Christ when He went after the Pharisees and the money lenders.

If we are aware of some of these biases, we can seek to correct them. We can begin to analyze as well as moralize. We can look at systems as well as individuals. We can take sides in specific struggles while still trying to love those we oppose.

We can do this because, as church people, we have some definite pluses on our side. One of these is the freedom we have in Christ. We are tied to no particular interest group so we can be open to new approaches and new points of view and follow the facts wherever they may lead. Also because we have dedicated ourselves to the service of others, we should be willing to do the tedious homework needed to really understand the "whys" behind so many of the problems we face.

THE PURPOSE OF THIS PAPER

The purpose of this paper is to say that many of the injustices we see all around us cannot be understood and dealt with effectively if we treat them in isolation one from another. It is something like dealing with the weather. If we want to explain why it is cloudy one day and then sunny the next, or why it snows in one place and rains in another, we have to know as much as we can about the weather *system*. The weather at different times and in different places is not simply a collection of isolated events. It is a whole. It is a system.

In the same way, a child dying of malnutrition in one of the slums of Rio, or a black steelworker out of work in Gary, or an important banker riding comfortably in his limousine down Park Avenue — these are not merely isolated events. They are related to and dependent upon one another. They are part of a system.

More specifically this paper contends that the system which creates and sustains much of the hunger, underdevelopment, unemployment and other social ills in the world today is *capitalism*. Capitalism is by its very nature a system which promotes individualism, competition and profit-making with little or no regard for the social cost. It puts profits and private gain before social services and human needs. As such, it is an unjust system which should be replaced.

In stating this quite strongly and in trying to prove it, it is our intention to raise this issue of capitalism as a legitimate and urgent topic for discussion.

The best way to do this, we feel, is to come to grips with certain myths about capitalism that hide its real nature from us. Again, it is like talking about the weather. As long as we think thunder is caused by Apollo clapping his hands, or lighting is a bolt of Zeus' getting even with one of his arch-rivals, we will never really understand what the weather system is all about. Myths serve a role in poetry and literature but not in trying to understand the vital issues of our day, the issues of world poverty, hunger, underdevelopment, racism, war, etc. For this we need facts, facts that shed light on the cause of some of these problems and how they can be dealt with.

In this paper we will respond to certain myths about capitalism, myths about its origins, its impact on the underdeveloped world, what it looks like and how it operates today, both in the U.S. and throughout the "free world." These are myths that are rarely articulated, much less challenged, in many of our church discussions on world justice and peace.

ORIGINS OF CAPITALISM

MYTH NO. 1: The first capitalist countries (England, France, the Netherlands, etc.) developed by pulling themselves up by their own boot straps.

FACT: England and other European countries developed largely because they had sea power to dominate the peoples and exploit the resources of newly-discovered lands. From the conquest and the pillage of Mexico and Peru by the Spaniards, to the sacking of Indonesia by the Portuguese and the Dutch, to the exploitation of India by the British, the early history of capitalist development is an unbroken record of international exploitation and consequent concentration of wealth in Western Europe.

It is estimated that over 500 million gold *pesos* were exported from Latin America between 1500 and 1600. The total wealth taken out of Indonesia by the Dutch East India Company for the period 1650-1780 amounted to more than 600 million gold *florin*. In 18th Century France, profits from the slave trade amounted to nearly half a billion *livres*. In the British West Indies, the profit from the labor of blacks during the same period amounted to over 300 million

pounds. Finally the result of the British plunder of India between 1750 and 1800 is estimated conservatively at 150 million pounds. In other words, the total amount taken by Western Europe from the rest of the world at the beginning stage of its "modern" development comes to over a billion pounds sterling, or more than the capital of all the industrial enterprises which existed in Europe around 1800!

Economists today talk about the necessity of large amounts of capital investment for an industrial economy to reach a point of "take-off," a point of sustained growth. The source of this capital for European industrial expansion came not only from the bitter exploitation of its own working class, e.g. the notorious sweat shops of Lancaster and the coal towns of South Wales, but, to an even greater extent, from the plundering of the human and natural resources of the rest of the world.

Neither, of course, was the development of capitalism in the U.S. free of such plunder. The fortunes of many of our first bankers, merchants, ship builders and plantation owners — i.e., the Pepperells, Cabots, Faneuils, etc. — were directly dependent on the slave trade. Others, such as John Jacob Astor, made millions in the fur trade, plying Native Americans with liquor and even paying others to kill them, to make the new territories of the West safe for trapping and "honest business." And the Robber Barons of the 19th Century not only used cheap Chinese and Filipino labor to build the great railroads that span our continent but matched their European counterparts in exploiting men, women and children in thousands of foundries and company towns throughout America, working people who had come to our shores "yearning to breathe free."

Indeed, while Europe had her colonies spread around the world, we had (even before the Spanish-American War of 1898 gave us Cuba, Puerto Rico and the Philippines) our own "internal colonies," made up of millions of black slaves, Native Americans and poorly paid workers, which generated the capital for our economic growth.

THE IMPACT OF CAPITALISM ON THE THIRD WORLD

MYTH NO. 2: The causes of underdevelopment in the poor countries of the "Third World" are: Ignorance, overpopulation, lack of natural resources and primitive, pre-capitalist economic structures.

FACT: The underdevelopment of the "Third World" is the direct result of its being incorporated, for the last 400 years, into the global capitalist system.

Overpopulation cannot be the cause of underdevelopment and poverty in the Third World since the highest densities of population occur, not in the poor countries, but in the rich, developed countries.

England has a population density of 586 square miles; West Germany, 606; Japan, 708; Belgium, 814; and the Netherlands, 938! The poor countries, by comparison, have relatively low densities of population. India has 415 people per square mile; the Philippines, 310; China, 197; Mexico, 62; Panama, 47; Brazil, 26; Tanzania, 25; Peru, 25; Paraguay, 12; and Gabon, 4!

Neither is the Third World lacking in natural resources. The two countries with the world's largest deposits of iron ore are India, with 21 per cent of the world's supply, and Brazil with 15 per cent. Oil, from Venezuela to Indonesia, is found in abundance. Copper, tin, zinc, bauxite, i.e. all the raw materials needed for modern, industrial societies, are equally plentiful. And agriculturally, from the pampas of Argentina to the Punjab of Pakistan, the poor countries have some of the richest and most fertile soil in the world, capable of feeding their populations many times over.

No, the misery and poverty found everywhere in the poor countries today is much more a result of oppression. Europe, beginning with Columbus, did not go out and find "underdeveloped" countries; she created them. For example, the so-called system of "mono-cultural production" (a one crop or one mineral export economy), described by western experts as the source of backwardness in the Third World, is not a system that dropped from heaven. It was brought and imposed by the Europeans on all their colonies in Asia, Africa, and Latin America. The sugar plant was brought by Columbus to the West Indies. Soon millions of slaves were brought from Africa to work the sugar plantations and cut the immensely profitable cane. Rubber was taken from Brazil to Southeast Asia, where Indians and Chinese provided cheap labor. Peanuts were brought from Brazil to West Africa and coffee from Arabia to Central and South America. The best lands, originally providing healthy diets for their inhabitants, were expropriated to produce cash crops for the European market. Malnutrition and starvation have been the lot of native peoples ever since. (A particularly notorious example of this was the Northeast of Brazil, originally one of the most fertile regions of South America. It was completely ruined by the ruthless exploitation of its soil by the Dutch and Portuguese sugar plantations of the 17th Century.)

Even in the area of manufacturing, it was the East which first provided finished goods for the more primitive economy of Europe. India in the 17th and 18th Centuries had a large textile industry based on cottage-type organization. With the development of cottonopolos in Manchester, and the need to export its production, English political domination resulted in the de-industrialization of India. Between 1815 and 1832 cotton exports from India fell 13 times. British imports to India increased 16 times. The maiming of the hands of thousands of Bengal weavers by British soldiers is an apt symbol of the whole process.

CAPITALISM AND THE THIRD WORLD TODAY

MYTH NO. 3: Increased foreign private investment, government loans from the rich countries and increased collaboration with the World Bank and other international development agencies is the only hope of development in the poor countries of the "Third World."

FACT: The strategy of the World Bank, western governments and multi-national corporations is one of self-interest. The strategy reinforces injustices in the internal structures of the poor countries. Even more it maintains a structure of neo-colonialism that provides for the rich nations privileged access to the raw materials and cheap labor of the Third World.

Poor countries are at the mercy of the developed countries mainly through their ever-increasing indebtedness. The external public debt by the end of 1976 for 96 developing countries was $227.4 billion, a 23 per cent increase over 1975, which was a 20 per cent increase over 1974.

Going back into the 1960s, we find that during the years 1962-1966, Latin America annually paid the United States $1.6 billion in debt service. This debt service exceeded all forms of economic assistance received from the United States during the same period.

One important reason for this growing indebtedness is the worsening terms of trade affecting the exports of the underdeveloped countries. This means that the poor countries are receiving less for their exports while they have to pay more for the goods they import from the rich countries.

The economies of most Third World countries rely heavily on export of one or two primary commodities (raw materials). While there have been occasional booms in primary commodity prices, both World Bank and United Nations Conference on Trade and Development (UNCTAD) indices show that terms of trade for the commodities covered (excluding petroleum) declined between 1953 and 1972 by about 2.2 per cent annually, on average.

Twelve major commodities account for roughly 80 per cent of the developing countries' export earnings. Between the mid-50s and the mid-70s these countries have increased the volume of their exports by more than 30 per cent, but their export earnings have risen by only 4 per cent. Consumers pay some $200 billion for these goods; producing countries receive only $30 billion of that total.

To take some of the worst examples: Between 1950 and 1973, the purchasing power of coffee exports went down 29.7 per cent; sugar exports bought 15.4 per cent less; and jute exports, 41.1 per cent less, in spite of the fact that prices for all these commodities increased. The meaning of these figures in daily reality is that in the early 1960s a truck could be imported into Tanzania for the earnings from five tons of cotton. In 1977 the same truck cost eight tons of cotton.

As developing countries try to maintain their imports (which often consist in consumer and luxury items for the wealthy landowners and industrialists who run the country) they seek increased foreign exchange by inviting in foreign private investments and negotiating new government or World Bank loans. But this merely adds salt to the wounds. The multi-national corporations soon begin to take out more in retained earnings, i.e. profits, than they originally invested and new loans from the World Bank and foreign aid programs only increase the debt.

In an attempt to offset this debt, occasionally the poor countries try to diversify their exports, especially in the area of manufactured goods, to bring in more foreign exchange. But these efforts are usually subverted by the developed countries who have the poor countries over an economic barrel. In 1966 Brazil set up its own factories for processing coffee and soon captured 14 per cent of the U.S. market. U.S. coffee manufacturers (Tenco, General Foods, Standard Brands, etc.) complained of "unfair competition." The U.S. government immediately threatened not to renew the International Coffee Agreement, which maintains stable prices, and to cut off aid. In 1968, Brazil gave in. It imposed an export tax on its own processed coffee and thus destroyed the fledgling industry.

Faced with the ever-increasing burden of debt, the poor countries have but one recourse. Following the "orthodox" economies imposed on them by the World Bank and the International Monetary Fund, i.e., that debt-serving and a balanced budget comes before economic growth, they cut their federal budgets and devalued their currencies. These are austerity measures that "stabilize" their economies. The victims of such "stabilization," of course, are not the wealthy elite, but the masses of the poor. Government spending for housing, education, health, and other non-productive programs is cut and the cost of living rises since the entire economy is heavily dependent on imports.

CAPITALISM AND THE DISTRIBUTION OF WEALTH IN THE U.S.

MYTH NO. 4: Reforms of the capitalist system within the United States have brought about a more equitable distribution of wealth and power among our people than ever before.

FACT: The distribution of wealth in the U.S. is almost identical with the distribution of wealth in India. The only difference is that in the U.S. the economic pie is much bigger and so the results of this maldistribution are not quite as visible. Furthermore, with this wealth goes much of the control over the country's resources, industry, and public services.

In 1941, two-thirds of all manufacturing assets in the nation were controlled by 1,000 large corporations. Thirty years later, through mergers and competition that smaller corporations could not withstand, only 200 giant corporations controlled the same percentage — by then amounting to a cool $350 billion.

Another aspect of this concentration of wealth and control is the growing role of the major banks. Of the 13,000 banks in the United States in 1970, four had over 16 per cent of all bank assets — Bank of America, Chase Manhattan, First National City Bank, and Manufacturers Hanover Trust; the top 50 had 48 per cent. Banks are also increasingly important in terms of corporate stock voting rights. A 1962 study indicated that 80 per cent of all corporate stock was owned by the top 1.6 per cent of the population. There is no evidence that this ratio does not still hold true today.

It is important, however, to know who has voting rights to stock, for that is where the real power lies. Such information is not easy to come by and a great deal remains unknown to the public. The conclusion of a 1978 Congressional study is that "voting rights to stock in large U.S. corporations are concentrated among relatively few bank trust departments (led by Morgan Guaranty Trust Co. of New York), insurance companies, mutual funds and their related investment advisory companies."

The 21 institutions which dominate the ranks of investors include 11 banks, five investment company complexes, four insurance companies and the Kirby Family Group which controls the world's largest investment company complex — Investors Diversified Services, Inc. The rapid growth of pension funds held in stocks is increasing the power of these and other large institutional investors who usually manage the funds. Management powers frequently include voting authority and the discretion to buy and sell. Pension fund stock already amounts to 37 per cent of all stocks held by all categories of institutional investors.

Not only is the wealth of the nation, i.e., the factories, utilities, banks, etc., largely owned by a very small percentage of the population, but the yearly national income is equally maldistributed. According to the Bureau of the Census, in 1978, the lowest fifth of families in the United States receives only 5.2 per cent of the national income while the highest fifth gets 41.5 per cent, or almost eight times as much.

An even more revealing way to look at the economy is through the influence and control which a mere handful of multi-billionaire families and financial groups have exerted for generations. The Rockefeller empire is not a thing of the past. Neither are the Dupont or Mellon trusts relics of another age. Again, precisely because these groups are anxious to keep the extent of their wealth from the public eye, accurate, up-to-date figures are not available. Studies from the 1930s through the 1970s have identified several groups looming on the economic horizon like elephants walking amidst ants. Although these groups regularly have interlocking interests in each other's area of influence, they are nevertheless distinguishable enough:

The Morgan Guaranty Trust Group, which includes in its sphere of influence General Electric, International Nickel, Standard Brands, Campbell Soup, Coca Cola, Upjohns, Mutual Life Insurance Co. of N.Y., etc.

The Rockefeller Group, which included Chase Manhattan Bank, Equitable Life Assurance Co., Standard Oil of N.J., Eastern Airlines, General Foods, Borden, etc.

The First National City Bank of N.Y. Group, which included Boeing, United Aircraft, Anaconda Copper, National Cash Register, etc.

The Mellon Group, which included Alcoa, Gulf Oil, Westinghouse, etc.

The Dupont Group, which included Dupont Chemical, U.S. Rubber, Bendix Aviation, etc. (The Duponts recently had to sell their controlling interest in General Motors stock due to a court order. But the proceeds were merely reinvested in high growth, frequently defense-related, industries.)

The Chicago Group, which unites many families, such as the McCormicks, the Deerings, the Nemours and the Fields, included the First National City Bank of Chicago, Continental Illinois National Bank, International Harvester, Sears Roebuck, Inland Steel, etc. Other families and groups, such as the Harrimans (Philadelphia), the Hannas (Cleveland), the Fords (Detroit), the Crockers (San Francisco), and the Hunts (Dallas) fill out the picture.

Although these families and groups compete with one another in trying to extend their spheres of influence, they also cooperate to run corporations that are too big for any one family or group to control. A good example is A.T.&T. On its board of directors are representatives of Chase Manhattan, First National City of N.Y., the Ford Foundation, the Chicago Group, and Morgan Guaranty Trust. It is truly a "collective possession" of the American upper class.

The effects of this concentration of wealth and power in the hands of a few are evident enough. A.T.&T., for example, is the largest private employer in the country, having over a million people on its payrolls. Forty-five per cent of its employees, however, are paid less than $7,000 per year (before taxes). What is particularly interesting is that only 4 per cent of Bell's white males earn so little whereas 64 per cent of all Spanish-surnamed employees, 79 per cent of all black employees, and 80 per cent of all female employees earn less than $7,000 annually. Indeed, the Equal Employment Opportunity Commission characterized A.T.&T. in 1971 as "without doubt the largest oppressor of woman workers in the U.S."

Does this mean that A.T.&T. is short on cash? Hardly. In 1970 A.T.&T. paid out more than $3 billion to stock and bond holders. In comparison labor costs only amounted to about $7 billion — out of a total annual revenue of $18 billion paid for by phone users all over the country. When we examine who owns the largest shares of A.T.&T. stocks and bonds, we find once again that it is the upper 1.6 per cent of the population. Maintaining this gravy train, then, even at the cost of rising rates and poor service to customers and blatant exploitation of women and minority groups is in the best interest of A.T.&T.'s corporate elite.

Many similar examples could be given, in practically every industry from textiles to steel, from meat packing to grave digging. Ultimately, however, the same simple fact emerges: Money is power. Indeed, the power of the financial oligarchy in the United States rests specifically on the fact that it commands most of the country's money capital. The bank assets controlled by the main financial groups mentioned above are twice as large as the annual budget of the Federal government. With this enormous wealth they dominate the American economy and determine its direction. Armed with the power to make key economic decisions concerning investments and the allocation of resources, they run their affairs and those of the nation according to the one rubric of corporate life: The maximization of profits.

CAPITALISM AND POLITICAL POWER IN THE U.S.

MYTH NO. 5: Despite the concentration of wealth in our country, we can trust in a democratically-elected government to work for the welfare of all the people.

FACT: The small elite that runs our economy also dominates political life, especially at the Federal level, making radical and far-reaching social reform almost impossible. Most members of the legislative and executive branches of the U.S. government are drawn from this financial elite and from the lawyers and economists who work for it. During the 90th Congress, the House of Representatives alone had 97 bankers, twelve of whom served on the House Banking Commission.

One way this group uses its political influence to maintain and even increase its slice of the national wealth is through its manipulation of the tax structure. Despite claims of "progressive taxation," the rich and super-rich have consistently provided themselves with legal gimmicks and loopholes to protect their huge fortunes. The result is that the burden of ever higher, more unjust taxes increasingly falls onto the backs of lower and middle income families.

These gimmicks and loopholes are well known: Oil depletion allowances, tax exempt bonds, capital gains, write-offs, executive expense accounts, farm subsidies, stock options, etc. Avoiding taxes and growing fat at the Federal trough is itself a big business. Here are a few examples:

In 1967, 21 millionaires paid no Federal taxes at all. In 1968, 155 persons with incomes exceeding $200,000 paid no taxes.

In 1972, 14 corporations paid an effective Federal corporate tax rate of less than 10 per cent and more than 1 per cent on $3.6 billion in taxable income. By 1976 the number of companies in this category had risen to 31 on an aggregate world-wide income of over $29.5 billion.

In 1976, the list of corporations paying *no income tax* included:
U.S. Steel
Bethlehem Steel
Armco Steel
National Steel
Republic Steel
Texas Gulf
American Airlines
Eastern Airlines
Pan Am
Pacific Gas and Electric
Chase Manhattan Corporation
Singer
Phelps Dodge
The Southern Company
Philadelphia Electric Company

These are but a few examples. They should help remind us that what we are dealing with in the United States, as Justice Douglas has said, is a system of socialism for the rich and "free enterprise" for the poor.

Not only do the wealthy use their political influence to manipulate the tax system for their own benefit but, through such groups as the Council on Foreign Relations (presently headed by David Rockefeller) and the Brookings Institute, they have great influence on the shaping of our foreign policy.

Their interest in foreign policy, of course, does not arise from some unique patriotic fervor. It is strictly determined by dollars and cents. By 1970, the book value of U.S. private corporate investment overseas exceeded $65 billion (it was only $11.6 billion in 1945) and was growing rapidly. In stimulating and protecting these lucrative investments the assistance of the government is indispensable. Foreign aid programs, for example, are used to secure concessions from weak foreign governments which fill the coffers of the multinational corporations.

When all else fails, of course, the corporate elite can resort to less subtle, more direct methods of persuasion. The invasion of the Dominican Republic by U.S. marines in 1965 is a classic example. The official reason was to prevent the island from going communist, though Juan Bosch, the popularly elected president deposed by the marines, was never a communist nor is he one today. The real reason was to protect the interests of U.S. big business, which has for generations made super-profits off the poverty of the Dominican people.

For example, the South Puerto Rico Sugar Co. (5 Hanover Square, N.Y.) whose board of directors intertwines with Rockefeller's Chase Manhattan Bank, gets two-thirds of its sugar from the

"GOD BLE$$ AMERICA!"

Dominican Republic. It had 120,000 acres in cane, 110,000 acres of pasture with choice livestock and 45,000 acres held in reserve (and economists wonder why the Dominican Republic has to import food from the U.S. to feed its own people!). It also owns a sugar mill, a furfural plant, a private railroad system and a dock and bulk sugar loading station.

In addition to this major investment, there was Alcoa Aluminum, owned by the billionaire Mellon family (852,000 tons of bauxite extracted in 1963, profits estimated at 47 per cent), United Fruit and the First National City Bank of N.Y.

Together, these investments provided huge profits for the American upper class. Because of the "successful" 1965 invasion, they still do today.

The evidence is clear, then, that in the United States we have a financial elite which exercises political influence far out of proportion to its size. This elite uses its power primarily for itself and secondarily, if at all, for the welfare of the majority of Americans.

CAPITALISM AND PATRIOTISM

MYTH NO. 6: To attack capitalism is unpatriotic; it is to attack the system that has made the United States great.

FACT: To attack capitalism is not unpatriotic for the simple reason that, as we have seen above, most U.S. citizens are not capitalists. The fact that, in a trillion dollar economy, we still have over 30 million people living in poverty and millions more with no real financial security (i.e. mortgages on homes, etc.) is striking proof that our economy is owned by and for a very small elite.

As U.S. citizens we are rightfully proud of our democratic traditions, traditions that uphold the rights of every individual to free speech, freedom of assembly, freedom of religion, etc. We believe in a government of the people, by the people and for the people. We are opposed, as Jefferson said, "to any form of tyranny over the mind of man." As a people, we agree that democracy, while maybe not the neatest and most efficient way to run a country, is still the best.

Because of this pride in democracy, however, when we approach issues of justice and peace we have a difficult time distinguishing democracy from capitalism. Democracy, after all, is a *political* system. It is a system where people vote for candidates who will represent them in government and rule them for a limited period of time. Capitalism, however, is an *economic* system where, for example, one individual owns a factory and hires others to work in it. While few people would deny that democracy is a good thing, capitalism is a horse of a different color. In fact, capitalism is the opposite of democracy, since it is an economic system not owned by the people and run for the people, but a system owned and run by a plutocracy, i.e., the rich

and super-rich.

Neither can we say that it is capitalism that has produced such great wealth in the United States. Those who have produced the wealth are the workers, blacks and whites, Greeks, Irish, Polish, and Chicano, generation after generation of hardworking men and women. And it is precisely these people, the working people of all races and creeds and nationalities, who have made this country great, who must constantly struggle even to gain a minimal share in the wealth they have produced, as if it did not belong to them in the first place.

A phrase we hear a lot about today is "community control." In many respects this would represent the best in democracy. Only when the people, both urban and rural, own their own land, their own factories, their own schools, their own banks, their own hospitals, and their own means of protection and law enforcement, will the vision of a truly democratic United States become a reality. In many respects, this is a modern day version of Jeffersonian democracy: A country made up of artisans and family farmers, each person owning a part of the assets of this great land and sharing equally in the fruits of his or her own labor.

But the direction of the economy today is just the opposite. Each year a quarter of a million family farmers leave their land because they can no longer compete with the huge corporate agri-businesses that are gobbling up the countryside and dominating the purchasing and distribution of farm produce. Each year thousands of small business operators close shop because they can no longer compete with the chain stores that undercut and outlast them. Each year hundreds of even medium and large companies are bought out and added to the growing list of subsidiaries of the huge conglomerates.

No, speaking against capitalism is not speaking against what made this country great. The people have made this country great and they deserve full democratic control over the economic as well as political aspects of their life.

CONCLUSION

We have looked, then, at some of the myths which prevent us from seeing clearly the nature of capitalism and how it really works. It is a myth that capitalism arose more from ingenuity than exploitation; that Asia, Africa and Latin America are only now becoming part of the global, "free enterprise," system; that development in underdeveloped countries can only be achieved through more foreign, private investment; that there is a fair distribution of wealth in the United States; that the interests of the corporate elite in the U.S. are synonymous with the interests of the people; that being against capitalism is unpatriotic. These are myths and they are false.

With these myths gone we can better see the roots of many of the injustices which face us today. Bloated stomachs, refugees, chronic unemployment, crowded urban ghettos, rising taxes, the breakdown of social services to the aged, the handicapped, the imprisoned, the lack of money for schools, hospitals, mass transit, and the continuance of imperialistic wars, etc., are all products of a system — a system which reaps excess for the few and scatters crumbs for the many.

As men and women thirsting for justice we are naive if we fail to take a hard, critical look at this system. If we do not do our homework, we might jump to the false conclusion that it is the average worker, the average parishioner, the average white suburbanite who is the culprit. We are more on the mark if we recognize that a common characteristic of the white workers, most women, Chicanos, blacks, farmers, Native Americans, office workers, etc., be they here in the U.S. or in other countries, is that they are exploited by the super-rich in a system designed to be unfair.

Our hope in writing this paper is to provoke discussions about capitalism and to urge U.S. church people to undertake a "radical" analysis of its effects upon the lives of U.S. citizens and people everywhere. In doing this we can learn from the Church in Latin America. For some years it has been grappling with the harsh effects of unjust economic and political systems. In 1968 at Medellin, Colombia, it clearly stated that many of the problems its people face are the results of a *system* — a system of internal colonialism and external neocolonialism.* As a result, the Church in Latin America is increasingly rejecting capitalism as a means to economic and human betterment and putting the gospel at the service of building a new kind of society.

We too need to explore the merits of an alterative system based not on competition and the profit motive, but on cooperation and solidarity. Socialism, by its definition, embodies these ideals and has, in a relatively short length of time, proven itself to be a viable alternative to capitalism. Granted, the specific form socialism would take in the United States, the richest country in the world, is an open question. But in light of all the serious problems we have in this country, such a discussion cannot be dismissed outright as naive, unpatriotic or even unchristian. Indeed, the burden of proof lies with those who say that capitalism here or in any country can serve the needs of the poor and the powerless. The fact is that, as we have seen, it has been and continues to be the principal cause of underdevelopment and poverty in the world today. ∎

*This position was reaffirmed at the Latin American bishops' meeting in Puebla in 1979.

The Fall of Capitalism

by Frank Cunningham

In a capitalist system the factories, mines and other major means of production are privately owned by people who employ others to do the actual work of producing "commodities" — products made not to be used by the producer but just to be sold. It was not Marx who discovered that the interests of workers and the interests of capitalists are opposed to one another in this system. Long before Marx was born, working people knew that their bosses would pay as little as possible in wages and squeeze as much work as they could out of their employees.

What Marx did was to study capitalism in its historical and social contexts to discover its strengths and its weaknesses. By this study he was able to show that capitalism was not accidental, but arose quite naturally in history; and he showed that it cannot survive. Thus Marx corrected a common error in thinking among many anti-capitalists of his time who believed that capitalism is like the devil — an unnatural moral deviation which working people had the bad luck of suffering from. At the same time, Marx listed the internal contradictions in capitalism that will lead to its downfall, in contrast to pro-capitalists who say that capitalism will last forever. In this chapter I will summarize the Marxist theory that explains why capitalism cannot survive.

The main internal contradiction of capitalism is that work is highly *social* or *collectivized*, while ownership is *private*. Under capitalism most people do not work alone or in small groups to produce things for private use or to trade for things made by others. People work in groups of hundreds or thousands, using sophisticated technology to mass produce commodities. This is a very powerful economic force. How production is organized has long-range effects on the whole of society. To be effectively and beneficially used, modern "socialized" labor needs

long-range, coordinated planning. But under capitalism the people who decide what and how much to produce, where to sell, how many to hire and fire, and so on, have very short-range interests — maintaining their private profits. The result is that the mighty force of modern industry is often used against the interests of the majority of people in the form of inflation, unemployment, overproduction, underproduction, useless and faulty goods, and so on. When economic crises occur, some of the smaller capitalists themselves are driven out of business.

To understand this contradiction better it is necessary to introduce some concepts of Marxist economic theory. There are many good summaries of Marxist economics, but here I will summarize only two points in order to explain why capitalism must fall.

LABOR THEORY OF VALUE

Since ancient times economic theorists have been puzzled by the question of why things can be exchanged for one another, or for particular amounts of money. Why is it that you can buy a pair of shoelaces, for instance, for approximately the same amount of money that you can buy a package of chewing gum, but not for anywhere near the amount of money you would need for a car? What determines the "exchange value" of commodities?

In the Middle Ages there was a theory of the "just price." Everything had a price set by God. By the 18th Century, when the science of economics was first developed, this theory was generally rejected. It did not explain how the Deity decided what the just price of everything was. Also, economists of that period felt that the medieval church, which was itself a major economic power, used the theory in a less than disinterested way when it interpreted "just prices."

Another theory was that commodities were exchanged according to the amount of gold they could be traded for. This didn't explain how gold received its value or why some things were exchanged for more gold than others. A more recent theory sug-

Frank Cunningham is an associate professor of philosophy at the University of Toronto. This abridged article is excerpted from his book, *Understanding Marxism*, Chapter 3. Reprinted with permission of Progress Books, 71 Bathurst St., Toronto, Ontario, Canada. Copyright © 1977 by Progress Books.

gested that things become more valuable or less valuable according to how badly people want them and how easy they are to get. If people want something because they badly need it and it is in short supply, they will be prepared to pay more for it and its value will rise. If people don't want something or if it is easy to obtain, then they will pay less, and its value will fall.

Marxists hold that this theory, called the theory of "supply and demand" helps explain the exact price something sells for in a particular time and place, but it still does not explain why things have the exchange values they do. Shoelaces always sell for less than cars, no matter how badly people want either and no matter what their supply. The theory also puts the cart before the horse, since one of the factors that affects how much people want things is how *valuable* those things are.

The theory of value Marx and Engels adopted was developed in the 18th Century by the Scottish economic theorist, Adam Smith. It is called the "labor theory of value." According to this theory, the exchange value of commodities is determined by the amount of labor, measured in working hours, necessary to make them (given current levels of technology). Shoelaces sell for less than cars, because it takes fewer people working fewer hours to make a pair of shoelaces than it does to make a car. Or, to put it another way, in the same period of time a person can make many more shoelaces than the same person could make cars. Adam Smith and other economists tested this theory by comparing prices of commodities with the necessary labor time involved in producing them. They found that while it does not explain the exact price of things, it does explain why they exchange for their approximate prices.

This theory takes the mystery out of the concept of value by relating exchange value to human labor. The value of a commodity is not some mysterious quality, but a characteristic it has in virtue of its relation to the work process that gives rise to it. Most of the early advocates of the labor theory of value were pro-capitalists, who were mainly concerned with using the theory to aid the fight against restrictions on trade and manufacture. Marx wished to deepen the theory to make it useful in working-class struggle.

THEORY OF SURPLUS VALUE

The economic system of capitalism is organized around the capitalist drive for private profit. Once it was understood that the value of a commodity came from the amount of labor in it, Marx asked the question: Where does profit come from? A capitalist can start with some raw materials, machines and employees, then manufacture commodities and sell them. And after paying wages and costs of materials and machines, he ends up with more money than he started with. How can this be? Various attempts by pro-capitalists to answer this question have failed. The popular view that profit comes from buying cheap and selling dear does not explain where capitalist profits come from. On the buying cheap and selling dear view, the one who gains through buying cheap does so because someone else loses either through selling cheap or buying dear. If a whole economy is taken into account, losses would, therefore, cancel out gains. The theory does not explain how capitalists acquire the money necessary to invest in production in the first place or how their profits continue to grow.

Marx's answer was that profit is possible because the capitalist pays less for the labor power of the workers he hires than they produce in commodity value. A worker sells his "labor power" — his ability to work measured in time — to a capitalist for wages. But the wages received for a certain number of hours of work represent a quantity of exchange value considerably less than the exchange value of the commodities produced during those same hours. For example, an auto-worker may receive $40 for eight-hours labor, but he may have produced engine parts totalling $90 in value during the same period of time.

A worker's labor power is itself a commodity, which he or she sells to a capitalist in exchange for

wages. The cost of this commodity is approximately what it costs to "reproduce" the worker's labor power itself. It is the cost of what is necessary to keep the worker alive, working and able to raise children who will be the next generation of workers. This cost is lower than the market cost of what is produced by that worker. (In North America today, Marxist economists estimate that the value of commodities produced is well over twice the value expressed by wages received for producing them.)

Marxists call the difference between these two amounts "surplus value." It is simply taken by the capitalist and used for things like paying rent or interest, investing in his own or other enterprises, and for his own survival and entertainment. The process of taking surplus value is called capitalist "exploitation." This process is at the heart of the capitalist economic system. Pro-capitalist economists from Marx's time to the present have expended tremendous energy trying to discredit this theory. Most of their arguments attempt to show that capitalists themselves create their profits.

Some people say that capitalists contribute to production by doing the "brain work" of management. One problem with this is that capitalists do not have to do any work (by brain or hand) if they don't want to, since they can hire people to do it. Moreover, the "brain work" that capitalists or their highly paid managers do most often does not contribute to the actual creation of commodities, but involves scheming ways to market goods, squeeze labor, or out-maneuver competition. Even if a capitalist did perform some useful function in production, his contribution to the finished product would be just that of one person among hundreds or thousands, whose combined and coordinated labors are all necessary.

Some say that capitalists derive their profits from the *risks* they have to take. This often-repeated claim has never had any weight. The mere fact of risk-taking does not create any exchange value, which is the same whether risks are taken or not. Usually, those who talk about the risks capitalists are supposed to take mean not that the risk creates value, but that because of taking risks, the capitalist deserves profits. In the first place, the Marxist theory of exploitation, as we shall see, is not a moral theory about who deserves what. But even if it were, why should risk-taking make one deserve profits? If the same goods could be produced more efficiently in a planned, socialist economy, without risking someone's individual investment, then the fact that capitalists defend a system where somebody has to take these supposed risks shows that they are either selfish or stupid, not that they deserve profits. Finally, what the capitalist presumably risks is his

original investment in a means of production. But this investment itself had to come from some place. It usually represents the profits gained by somebody, and therefore has its source in the surplus value created by labor.

CAPITALIST PRODUCTION

Of course there is much more to Marxist economic theory, but this summary of capitalist exploitation will serve to show how Marx analyzed the unsolvable problem capitalism faces. A common misinterpretation of Marx's analysis is that he thought capitalism would fall because it is not fair or just. Now while Marx's discovery of the source of profit does explain the truth behind a long-standing socialist view that "capitalism is theft," Marx did not hold that capitalism would fall because it is unfair. It will fall because the capitalist system itself creates problems it cannot solve.

The production of commodities for profit is possible only when labor is collectivized. That is, it requires that a great number of people do specialized jobs using advanced machinery so as to produce the most goods in the least time. The constant pressure of competition ensures that capitalists cannot lag behind in the production of commodities. It also ensures that they must strive to keep wages down as far as possible. They lay workers off whenever keeping them on cuts into profits. (This is doubly advantageous to them, since having unemployed workers around is a threat to other workers and helps to keep wage demands down.) They also keep prices up as high as they can get away with, even *above* their exchange value if possible. These things are obviously not in the interests of working people.

There are other problems. Working people are the ones who produce commodities, but they are also the main consumers. However, since working people are not paid enough to purchase all they produce (and capitalists cannot consume what is left without cutting into profits), there are regular crises of "overproduction," where there are too many goods on the market compared to people's ability to pay for them. In extreme cases these crises become depressions. In less extreme cases they are now called "recessions," such as the protracted one we have been experiencing in Canada. An important discovery of Marx was that these crises are not accidents or the result of bad management, but are a natural outcome of the capitalist system.

Crises are marked by a general dropping off of production, with resulting layoffs and the bankruptcy of smaller capitalist firms. In the early stages of capitalism these crises often led to a drop in prices, though this did not help working people, since they also led to higher unemployment and lower wages.

Capitali$m is when they decide how valuable we are.

(speech: ALL RIGHT... NOW EVERYONE IS IN HIS OR HER RIGHTFUL PLACE...)

LIBERATION NEWS SERVICE

More recently, capitalists have learned to dampen some of the effects of crises through things like unemployment insurance. But in another way crises today are more severe than earlier ones, since they are marked by *both* growing unemployment *and* rising prices. This is due primarily to the fact that giant monopolies today are in a better position to price fix than before. Marx predicted that these crises would occur at 10-year intervals and that the intervals would grow shorter as capitalism nears its end. His predictions are proving correct.

Many other problems are created by the capitalist economy, and the ones I have mentioned have many more facets. Those who wish to pursue these topics might want to read one of the several Marxist texts on the subject or read Marx's famous *Capital*, where the mechanics of the capitalist economic system are discussed in detail.

Marx described capitalist production as "anarchy." This does not mean that individual capitalists are crazy or irrational, but that the entire system, motivated as it is by competition for private profit, creates more problems than it can solve. In talking about the anarchy of capitalist production, Marx was contrasting it to what he saw would be possible in a socialist, planned economy where collectivized mass production is organized so as to serve the best long-range interests of the working people themselves. In socialist economies there are no economic crises, and needless to say there are no policies to create unemployment or keep wages down. Under a system of private ownership, this sort of planning has no place.

THE WORKING CLASS

The working class is made up of those people who do not own any means of production but sell their ability to work to those who do. The most important

conclusion Marx drew from his analysis of capitalism is that it is the working class that can and will lead successful socialist revolutions. In this view, Marxists differ from those who see socialist revolutions led by a few individuals, or as a rising of all groups in society against capitalism without any group playing a leading role, or as the result of capitalists themselves becoming "enlightened" and handing over power. The contradiction between collectivized labor and private ownership is expressed as the contradiction between capitalists and the working class.

The system of capitalist commodity production brings the working class into existence. But in doing so, capitalism also creates a force that eventually destroys the capitalist system itself. As Marx and Engels put it, capitalism creates its own "grave diggers." The Marxist basis for this view is that because of its mode of work, the working class is provided with both the *ability* to lead a successful revolution and also the *incentive* to want one.

Workers have the incentive to change the social and economic system of capitalism for several reasons. Even working people with relatively high wages cannot afford the luxuries taken for granted by capitalists and their overpaid managers. In a system geared to private profit, life for most working people is hard. Apart from monotonous, tiring and unrewarding work, workers face the constant pressure of job insecurity. One's old age is not adequately provided for. A working person has practically no say in the safety of his or her work conditions, much less in how work is organized or what is produced.

Through work, working-class people also acquire the ability to change this oppressive system. Industrialization forced people off farms and out of small shops and into cities and large factories. Industrialized work creates the habits and skills of collectivity

... I don't care what they say about our economy, it still ain't no Great Depression ...

... It's a Very Good Depression, but it ain't no Great Depression ...

hereth.

and discipline. Knowing how to work consistently in a coordinated way does not come automatically to people. Depending on their class background and type of job, some never learn these things. Large-scale industries and offices train workers in these skills. These are potentially revolutionary abilities. The main force standing in the way of socialism is the capitalist class, which is small in number but controls weighty instruments of power, such as the army and the police. To compensate for this advantage, the rest of society must be able to move in a collective, united and disciplined way.

Through its regular work, there is another advantage gained by the working class. At least in its industrial sector, the class has its hands on the actual means of production. It has the ability to stop the wheels of production and also to turn them on again. Not only do workers have some direct power over the capitalists, but they learn that they can challenge capitalists and make gains in their own interests. This is important, because capitalists try to make working people feel powerless and unsure of themselves.

Early in its history the working class learned that it has these abilities and strengthened them through the formation of unions. The value of working-class unity and collectivity makes itself felt when workers cooperate in strikes, refuse to cross picket lines or support other issues. These skills are crucial to winning a revolution and building a socialist society. And the working class learns them in a kind of on-the-job training program unwittingly provided under capitalism.

The Marxist view about the central revolutionary role of the working class has come under fire from several directions. One criticism is that the peasantry

is the key revolutionary class. Another is that the working class has "sold out." We will look at these criticisms in turn.

PEASANTS AND INDUSTRIAL WORKERS

Russia and China had large peasant populations, that is, poor farmers whose families used almost all they produced. More recently peasants and landless farmworkers have been active in Third-World liberation struggles. These facts have led some to conclude that Marx and Engels were wrong to see industrial workers as the key to revolutionary change.

One problem with the concept of peasant leadership is that it overlooks some very important additions to the theory of Marxism since it was first advanced over a century ago. The most important of these concerns *imperialism*. In the late 19th Century and throughout the 20th Century, industrialized capitalist countries such as England, the United States, France, Japan and others began wholesale capitalist expansion into other parts of the world. Either by direct military invasion or by installing puppet governments, they forced large parts of the world to provide cheap labor and raw materials for them and to serve as a captive market for manufactured goods at inflated prices.

Africa, Asia, South and Central America, Russia and Eastern Europe were quite consciously divided up by the big industrial powers. The economic gains were great and in some cases almost certainly staved off revolutions at home by bailing out the home economy and stemming discontent.

The effect of imperialism on non-industrialized parts of the world was to create revolutionary potential there. In some cases imperialism introduced a measure of heavy industry, which created the beginnings of a militant industrial working class. But even in those countries where little industry was developed, the nature of farm work itself began to change as peasants were forced to become farmworkers on large plantations owned by other people, usually European colonial settlers. This created another economic shift as small-scale, variety crop production gave way to large-scale single commodity production (of such products as coffee, tobacco or sugar).

Earlier I suggested that incentive and the ability to change the system were qualities of the industrial working class that make it the key force in revolutionary change. Where peasant forces have been instrumental in revolutionary movements it is because imperialism has forged similar qualities in them. The peasantry does the work; someone else makes the profit. Agricultural and plantation work in imperialized countries is highly collectivized and disciplined. Where peasant forces play a revolutionary role it is not because Marx and Engels were wrong about the revolutionary nature of the working class, but because imperialism has created some important working-class qualities in the peasantry.

WORKING CLASS 'SELLOUT'?

The North American media have created the image of the industrial worker as a bloated and complacent person who has a stake in maintaining the present social system. This image has prompted some to suggest that while the working class may have had revolutionary potential in the 1930s, it has now been "bought off" and has chosen instead to support capitalism. There are two questions here: Is the working class bloated? And has it sold out?

If someone measures a person's well-being against a standard of complete poverty — starvation, rags for clothing, no roof over one's head — then I suppose that most North American industrial workers are well off. But this is not a realistic standard. Well-being should be measured against what is possible. In a land rich in natural resources and industrial potential, it is not necessary for working people to have to pay from 25 per cent to 50 per cent of their income on housing. Inflation should not make each year's paycheck worth less than before. Even with a high-paying job, how well off is someone if that job could be taken away at any time? In fact only some working people have high-paying jobs.

The view that the working class has sold out is heard more in North America than in other parts of the world. In Europe, working people in countries like France and Italy swell the ranks of revolutionary parties that may be on the eve of transforming those countries to socialism. What is the difference between the working classes of those countries and of Canada or the U.S.? On the "sell-out" theory, the difference must be that the North American worker is too cowardly or too stupid or too immoral to risk leading society in revolutionary change.

Marxists maintain that this theory rests on a wrong view about how people come to have the attitudes they do. It supposes that at some point members of the North American working class came to the realization that socialism is an alternative and revolution requires working-class leadership, but then they deliberately chose to turn their back on socialism.

Revolutionary consciousness and determination do not come and go in such a haphazard fashion. It is not a matter of an effort of will. To think that having or abandoning revolutionary consciousness is a matter of individual choice is to view things in a narrowly moralistic way. Sometimes I suspect that people who hold the sell-out theory confuse worker militancy in strikes with *revolutionary* militancy: Since North American workers are quite militant trade unionists, it is assumed that they must also be revolutionaries. Then when they don't organize in large numbers for revolution, the conclusion is drawn that they have sold out.

There are definite conditions that lead to revolutionary consciousness. These include economic conditions, the effectiveness of anti-revolutionary propaganda, the nature and extent of working-class political organizations, the success of divide-and-conquer tactics, and so on. Largely because of the success of imperialism, important sectors of the North American working class were spared the worst economic pressures, and this meant that they did not look for solutions to their problems outside of the capitalist system. This has, indeed, been one of the many bad effects of imperialism. The task of the scientific socialist, however, is not to berate working people for not being revolutionary, but to discover just what conditions lead to revolution and what conditions hold it back.

CAN CAPITALISM BE SAVED?

To summarize, the Marxist claim is that capitalism has created economic forces it cannot control, much less direct for the benefit of everybody in society. At the same time capitalism has brought into existence the modern working class, which *can* control and direct those forces. But it can only do so by a socialist transformation of society, which ends the system of capitalist exploitation altogether. Thus capitalism digs its own grave.

Some people maintain that while this may have been true of the "classic" capitalism Marx was writing about, capitalism has now changed in ways that make it stronger, and capitalists have taken measures to avoid socialist revolution. Thus, they say that capitalism can be saved. Marxists do not deny that capitalism has changed and that capitalists use their considerable power to fight socialism. However, the internal problems of capitalism cannot be overcome in the long run, and measures taken to avoid socialism can only set it back temporarily. I will conclude by looking at five things that are often said to be able to save capitalism.

IMPERIALISM

Advanced capitalism turns into its imperialist phase. By forcing people in other parts of the world to work at starvation wages, capitalists increased profits and were able to yield to some of the workers' demands in their home country for higher wages. By creating captive markets in other countries, capitalists had places to sell goods at inflated prices and to dump goods when there were crises of overproduction at home.

Does imperialism, then, save capitalism? Some have maintained that it does. They note that Marx and Engels predicted a probable socialist revolution in England or Germany in the last century. But due to imperialist ventures, these revolutions did not take place, and hence, it is argued, Marx's whole theory is shown to be false. The failure of this prediction has shown that there were inadequacies in the theory, but it did not show that the theory is wrong. Lenin

would snap first at its "weakest link," which he considered his own native Russia. The Russia of that time was both an imperialist power, caught up in a costly and destructive war between imperialist rivals for markets (World War I), and at the same time it was subject to the imperialist domination by stronger capitalist countries. Taking these factors into account, it should not be surprising that the first socialist revolution was in Russia and the other nations that make up the USSR. Similarly, China, Cuba, North Korea and, for the most part, the

IN A NUTSHELL...

THE GOVERNMENT REDUCES CORPORATE TAXES TO ENCOURAGE INVESTMENT AND CREATE JOBS.

PRICES RISE... CORPORATE PROFITS INCREASE

EVERYWHERE RICH CORPORATIONS CLAMOR TO REDUCE PRICES

AND THE CONSUMER LIVES HAPPILY EVER AFTER.

wrote an important book on this subject called *Imperialism, the Highest Stage of Capitalism* in which he shows how imperialism is a natural outgrowth of capitalism — one that does temporarily solve some problems, but that can only postpone revolutions in the major capitalist countries, not prevent them.

The difficulty imperialism created was to move the problems of capitalism to new territory. In fact it moves it to territory less advantageous to the capitalists. By super-exploiting workers in countries subject to imperialist rule, it creates even greater incentive for revolution. Imperialism also sparks nationalistic sentiments. At home imperialists can flag wave and urge their own working class to go along with them for the sake of their common country (a cynical ploy, since capitalists don't care about the real needs of their countries). In the nations they subject to imperialist plunder, capitalists are correctly regarded as foreign invaders who have no business there at all. Imperialism has made it relatively easy for forces of national liberation and revolution, such as the NLF in Vietnam, to rally large segments of the population to the anti-imperialist struggle.

Taking imperialism into account, Lenin predicted that capitalism, regarded on a worldwide scale,

countries of Eastern Europe, all of which are now socialist, were subject to the most devastating imperialist rule. It is because of imperialism also that national-liberation struggles in Africa, Latin America and Asia often move quickly in a socialist direction.

MONOPOLIZATION

Competition is a major source of capitalist economic problems. Why cannot capitalists eliminate competition through creating monopolies? Monopolization has indeed helped many capitalists. Groups of capitalist concerns form monopolies (or, what comes to the same thing, "cartels" or "conglomerates") that fix prices and remove some of the pressure of competition. Every time there is an economic crisis, smaller capitalist enterprises go under, leaving larger and larger ones to corner the market even further.

Still, monopolization will not save capitalism. In the first place, like imperialism, it creates special problems of its own for the capitalist system. Capitalist ownership of the means of production cannot become concentrated in fewer hands without more and more smaller capitalists going out of business. This has the effect of forcing more discontented people into the working class, and it makes it harder to maintain the myth that anybody with enough intelligence and drive can be a capitalist.

Theoretically, I suppose one could imagine a single world monopoly which could afford to pay higher wages and improve working conditions, because it had no fear of competitors who by keeping wages down would be able to produce competitive products for less. But think of how unlikely such a development really is. It would not be enough for some capitalists to gain a monopoly in just one industry. They would have to monopolize *all* industries. If someone monopolized the entire auto industry and then stopped making improvements in auto-manufacturing machines, what is to prevent an enterprising manufacturer in some other industry from using his profits to invest in new and better auto-making machines, thus becoming a competitor of the auto monopoly? This sort of industry jumping is not at all unusual in capitalism.

Not only would capitalists have to monopolize all industries, they would have to monopolize the whole world. Capitalists do not care about state boundaries. They are prepared to make profits wherever they can manufacture goods the cheapest and sell them at the highest prices. But even if this imaginary world monopoly *could* have been created, it is now too late, because capitalists have to contend with competition from the socialist countries, which do not have economic crises and are becoming more and more economically powerful each year.

In the U.S., where monopolization has developed quite far, there is still vicious rivalry among *different* groups of large capitalists, who still have all the characteristics that mark the anarchy of capitalist production. Monopolization is only beneficial to some capitalists in the short run. And it does not change the fact that modern production has outgrown a private-profit economy. The dream (or nightmare) of a single world monopoly is so far from reality that it is hardly worth considering.

STATE INVOLVEMENT

In the early days of capitalism, most pro-capitalists argued that the government ought to play a very small role in the economy. At that time they wanted to break the government-church-feudal network which had attempted to constrain manufacture and trade. Now, even if they pay lip service to this philosophy, the largest capitalists all promote active government involvement in the economy. This is because they see that governments can help them to weather crises and make profits. In some capitalist countries the government plays a larger role than in others, but in all capitalist countries, government involvement in the economy is on the increase.

Pro-capitalist governments help ease crises by making loans and tax gifts to businesses and by controlling wages. They purchase expensive goods, such as military equipment, from corporations at inflated prices. They help corporations to market their goods. For instance, the Canadian government helps Canadian-based war-goods producers to market their wares through the Canadian Commercial Corporation (a Crown corporation formerly called "War Supplies Limited").

Pro-capitalist governments finance the research for new technology, which is then used by capitalists in production. Sometimes governments run some industries for the capitalists. Occasionally people talk of countries like England as if they were socialist because the government owns and runs some major industries (such as the English coal industry). In fact, some essential industries are no longer profitable, so the government manages these industries for the capitalists.

Useful as state regulation of portions of the economy can be for capitalists, it cannot save the system of capitalism. The main problem is that the government has to find the money to do all these things somewhere. If government projects were financed by the capitalists, their profits would fall, which is just what government involvement in the economy is supposed to prevent. Therefore all capitalist governments leave giant loopholes in their corporate tax structures, and the state gets its money from working people. But higher taxes just create more discontent and further lower people's ability to purchase goods.

State regulation of the economy in the interests of capitalists has a two-edged effect on people's attitudes toward government. On the one hand, by trading on the capitalist-inspired myth that any government regulation is a form of socialism, it confuses people about what socialism is and makes them cynical. If this is socialism, who needs it? On the other hand, it opens the door to some economic reforms that people can force the government to make. For instance, working people can force the government to enact legislation setting minimum wages or regulating working conditions, which they could not do if the government played no role in economic matters at all. Even if these reforms are minor, relative to people's needs, they help them to learn what *could* be done if there was a workers' government that ran the entire economy in their own interests.

THREATS OF VIOLENCE

A time-honored method of oppressive regimes is to try keeping people down by threatening them with job loss, prison or even death if they try anything revolutionary. Capitalism is no exception. During the 1919 Winnipeg General Strike, which was put down with horses, clubs and guns, workers learned that capitalists are prepared to use police against the people. The lesson has been repeated many times in Canadian working-class history. How far can the threat of jail or harassment go in preventing people from challenging the capitalist system?

Obviously threats have some effect. Any sane person thinks twice before taking risks. But I do not think that threats of violence can save capitalism any more than they have saved any of the oppressive systems that preceded it. If history has taught us nothing else, it has taught us that there are limits to how far

people can be bullied. Look at situations where the threats and actual use of violence have been extreme.

Portuguese people lived under the systematic terror of fascism for 48 years. Now we learn that the Communist Party there was actively organizing underground the whole time at tremendous risk and had a membership of around 30,000 just before the 1974 anti-fascist coup.

I heard a priest from the U.S. who had been locked up in the prisons of Vietnam tell of Vietnamese women who were brought out every morning and told that if they didn't salute the U.S. flag and the flag of its puppet government, they would be beaten and then put into the infamous "tiger cages" (rooms about four feet square). He reported that almost to a woman they refused to salute those symbols of imperialism. There is a point where human dignity rebels at the brutality of intimidation.

MIND CONTROL

Through the school system and the pro-capitalist news and entertainment media, working people are subjected to a daily barrage of propaganda designed to convince them that capitalism is good, that socialism is evil, that you can't change things, that the real source of your problems is the working people of another race or nationality or sex, or that you, yourself, are to blame for your problems. There are any number of other ideas designed to confuse working people about what is wrong and how to change things. Of course, many people in educational and cultural institutions are themselves honestly confused about the source of their problems and pass on the theories they have learned. Nevertheless, such propaganda dampens revolutionary class consciousness and hence helps to perpetuate capitalism.

Effective as capitalist mind-control techniques are, there are limits to how long they can save capitalism. People who have already participated in socialist revolutions were all subjected to pro-capitalist propaganda, as were the working people and their allies all over the capitalist world who are now engaged in anti-capitalist struggles. Why cannot others overcome the effects of this propaganda too? It is typical of the elitist thinking of the bourgeoisie to regard working people as fools and sheep who can be convinced of anything. In fact, life itself has a way of revealing truths and exposing lies. ∎

Group Exercise

Your group will need newsprint and markers or a chalk board and chalk. One group member should assume leadership for this exercise and serve as time keeper and facilitator. (It is assumed that prior to this exercise participants will have read the two texts.) The exercise is designed for a two hour period, which is to be divided into three parts: Discussion of Readings (30 minutes); Signs of the Times (45 minutes); General Discussion (45 minutes).

Discussion of Readings (30 minutes)

To facilitate this discussion, time should be given to each participant to complete the following statements with brief answers. These first three statements should take about 15 minutes.

1 Two things I learned from today's readings:

2 After reading the texts, I have these two questions:

3 I disagree with the readings on the following two points:

Devote the last 15 minutes of this portion of your session to role play answers to the following:

You have been asked to explain to someone in your congregation the concept of "Labor Theory of Value." Using an example of two different products (*e.g.*, cars and shoelaces as Cunningham does) how would you explain it? How would you explain the difference between the Labor Theory of Value and value based on supply and demand?

Signs of the Times (45 minutes)

Have on the wall a series of newsprints with the following headings:

Signs that the system isn't working:	**1** Who is being exploited? **2** Who benefits? **3** Are working people aware of this exploitation?
	4 If so, how? If not, why not? **5** What signs of organized efforts do we see confronting these injustices? **6** Are we as persons or as a parish involved in these organizations? If so, how? If not, why not?

Have participants brainstorm about signs that indicate the system isn't working for people. Be as specific as possible in describing these signs. List the signs on the appropriate newsprint.

Select two of these signs that everyone would like to analyze a little more carefully from a systemic point of view. Single these two out for special attention.

Proceed to the next questions. Analyze first one sign and then the second, so that the process of asking the six questions is completed twice. Remember, the key to this exercise is to have all participants be as specific as possible with their answers, having them indicate by name, if necessary, persons, groups, agencies, organizations, etc. that are called for.

How does our perception of each "sign that the system isn't working" change from when we merely listed it to when we analyzed it? Do we feel more or less hopeful or capable of dealing with it?

Many people believe that unemployment, inflation, inadequate health care facilities, poor housing and a decrease in the real wages of the average worker, along with those other *signs* that we have listed indicate that our system is not working. Profits are high but money is not spent on providing adequate human services. For example, during the first quarter of 1979, at a time when all of us were feeling the pinch of increased food and gasoline costs, McDonald's Corporation profits were up 17 per cent; General Electric, 22 per cent; Exxon, 37 per cent; Chase Manhattan Bank, 60 per cent; Mobil Oil, 81 per cent and Standard of Ohio, 302 per cent.

General Discussion (45 minutes)

After the group has read and reacted to the above paragraph, move on to the following reading and discussion question for the remainder of the time period.

"A socialist society is one in which the major means of production and distribution (factories, mines, large food and clothing chains, and so on), as well as financial institutions like the banks are owned and controlled by the working people of that society." — Cunningham, *Understanding Marxism*

We have seen that in many ways more and more of us working people are experiencing the alienating consequences of not being involved in making decisions at our work places. That area of our life in which we spend most of our time and creative energy is beyond our control and involvement. What does this say about the growing gap between democracy, our political system which stresses citizen involvement, and capitalism, our economic system which centralizes the decision-making process in the hands of a few owners?

If socialism is as described above, why is there so much hostility in this country to the concept? Does socialism threaten democracy, or does it threaten capitalism?

"THOSE WHO PROFESS TO LOVE FREEDOM AND YET DEPRECATE AGITATION

are those who want crops without plowing. This struggle may be a moral one, or it may be physical, but it must be a struggle. Power concedes nothing without a demand. It never did, and never will."
— Frederick Douglass (1857)

SESSION 4

The Elements of Class

You might not be responsible for being down, but you gotta be responsible for picking yourself up.

Over the years this has been a commonplace notion among U.S. workers — especially immigrants, national minorities and women — in search of the American dream. And after examining the system called capitalism in the last session, it now becomes necessary to examine the U.S. class structure to determine what chances the unemployed have of "picking themselves up." One commentator put it another way, "We should judge the success of a country not by the amount of millionaires it produces but by the number of poor people it contains within its borders."

Even in international and foreign policy, the concept that the United States could help countries "pull themselves up by their own bootstraps" was idealistically applied in titles such as "Operation Bootstrap," the economic plan to put Puerto Rico back on its feet in the 1950s and 1960s. It was a dismal failure. Some 40 per cent of the population now live outside Puerto Rico, and of those who remain more than half are on food stamps.

Why can't the unemployed pick themselves up? Why are the developing countries unable to "make it" on their own?

In 1848, two men opened a famous document on the subject this way: "The history of all hitherto existing society is the history of class struggles." The men were Karl Marx and Friedrich Engels, and the document was entitled *The Communist Manifesto*. The *Manifesto* has been called the most influential document of modern times and, after the Bible, one of the most widely read.

"Marx," said H. G. Wells, "who did not so much advocate the class war, the war of the expropriated mass against the appropriating few, as foretell it, is being more and more justified by events."

Which puts us up against the question: What is this thing called *class*? The temptation is to think in three categories: Upper, middle and lower, with most people positioning themselves in the middle, reasoning, "We know we're not rich, and who wants to call themselves lower class?"

But a more scientific way of looking at class is to ask what role people play in production, in decision making, in control over what they do

for a living. Consider, for example, Maurice Zeitlin's comment on white collar employees in the "Who Owns America?" selection for this session:

"Beneath their nice clean collars (if they wear them at all) they are propertyless workers, entirely dependent for their livelihoods on the sale of their capacity to work. And this is the essence of working class reality."

Whoever can identify with the words, "dependent for their livelihoods on the sale of their capacity to work," and who are deprived of control over their work and the products of their work, are, plain and simple, working class, or non-owners.

This is one way to understand class consciousness. The fundamental differences by which people earn (or do not earn) a living — some by working, some by owning — in the end creates classes with fundamentally different and, in many respects, antagonistic attitudes and aspirations. These classes, with their conflicts and struggles, comprise the rise and fall of human progress.

Class consciousness motivates people to join in the struggle with others to build a better society, but this cannot be done unless workers see each other as equals. Factors such as racism and sexism dehumanize people, lead them to think of others as inferior, and greatly inhibit progress.

Under the capitalist system, capitalists compete for profits and workers compete for jobs. Some people believe that this is just the way things are. This fatalistic acceptance of the order of things (many times thought to be a divine order, or at worst, a result of Original

Sin) prevents us from seeing our personal histories in the larger context of the political and economic system in which we live.

It is not difficult to see how some people think this is how it must always be. Unemployed people are pictured as drones, or ''sponges on welfare'' who have only themselves to blame for being jobless. (In fact, unemployed people are part of the working class for whom capitalism does not provide jobs.) Working people frequently attribute the success of big business and government figures to their intelligence and courage, and tend to blame themselves for their own failure to get ahead. Clearly there is a need for consciousness-raising.

The final two selections in this session attempt to locate the churches in class struggle. Third World liberation theologian Gustavo Gutierrez sees the relationship between owners and non-owners in terms of oppressor and oppressed. He points out that to speak of class struggle is not to advocate it, but simply to recognize it as fact. And he continues:

''For the ecclesial community to recognize the fact of class struggle and to participate actively in it will not be a negation of the message of unity it bears; rather, it will be to discover the path by which it can free itself from that which prevents it from being a clear and true sign of brotherhood and sisterhood.''

Frances Fox Piven takes up the question, ''What is the role of the Church in a system that is dysfunctional for the poor?'' She concludes that ''the transforming power of the gospel is not likely to achieve its greatest effects in its attempts to transform the wealthy. Rather, the transforming power of the gospel, if it is truly to be a nourishing and vigorous force, ought to orient itself to the poor, to the working people who are victims of wealth and power.'' Her words imply that there is a choice to be made: Which side are you on? ∎

Who Owns America?

by Maurice Zeitlin

Do you remember those full-page newspaper ads that showed a little old lady stroking *her* locomotive, supposedly owned by millions of ordinary Americans just like her? Or Standard Oil's gushing claim, "Yes, the people own the tools of production. . . . How odd to find that it is here, in the capitalism [Karl Marx] reviled, that the promise of the tool has been fulfilled." Well, it's happening again.

A Texaco television commercial has Bob Hope asking us to "take a look at the owners of America's oil companies," and then leading us on a tour of a typical community made up of just plain folks like you and me. A recent book, received with much fanfare in the press, repeats the refrain. Its author, longtime management consultant and publicist Peter Drucker, tells us that an "unseen revolution" has wrought "a more radical shift in ownership than Soviet communism." Even more amazing, "the socialism of Marxist theory has been realized for the first time on American soil."

Not only are the means of production now in everyone's hands, but the U.S. Chamber of Commerce confides that the United States has become a "post-industrial society." College textbooks inform us that a "dramatic shift from blue collar to white collar, from brawn to brain [has] occurred," and the best-seller *Future Shock* rhapsodizes that "for the first time in human history," a society — *our* society — has "managed within a few short decades to throw off the yoke of manual labor." A book on "power in America" celebrates the passing of classes and suggests that we organize popular visits to "Newport, and bus tours through Grosse Pointe, for purely educational purposes — like seeing Carlsbad Caverns once." It is time, the author advises us, to shout, "The Working Class is dead. Long live the memory of the Working Class." And, summing it all up, a popular book on how to be a politician announces that "the economic class system is disappearing. . . . Redistribution of wealth and income . . . has ended economic inequality's political significance."

So, what has happened to classes? Who does own America, and how has it all been changing? Has the capitalist class really been "lopped off" at the top, as Harvard's Talcott Parsons once pithily put it? Has the ownership of American corporations become so dispersed that control has shifted to "professional managers" who are merely the "trustees" for all of us — "stockholders, employees, suppliers, consumers, and the public" — as Donald S. McNaughton, the chairman of Prudential Life, announced in a recent speech? Has the yoke of manual labor really been lifted? Is the working class now a mere memory? Or are the claims that prompt these questions really pseudofacts that are as plausible and persuasive as they are deceptive? The answer, I think, is clear: Economic inequality weighs as heavily and cuts as deeply as ever, and neither capitalists nor workers have vanished from American life.

Let's look first at who owns what. It's certainly hard enough to find out, even if, like Government economists, you have access to Internal Revenue Service (IRS) data. No law requires Americans to report their net worth, and besides, wealth is deliberately hidden, whether out of modesty or to avoid taxes. Still, an ingenious method of estimating wealth has been devised, to make the dead disclose what the living conceal. It is called the "estate multiplier technique," and it uses IRS data on estate tax returns. It treats those who die in any year as a "stratified sample" of the living on whose estates tax returns would have to be filed if they died during the year — that is, those with estates worth $60,000 or more. All told, only 4 per cent of the adults in this country have estates as large as $60,000, counting *everything* they own, including cash in hand or under the mattress, and the mattress itself. But within that group, a minute number of Americans make up the real owners of America.

Maurice Zeitlin is a professor of sociology at the University of California, Los Angeles. Reprinted by permission from *The Progressive*, 408 West Gorham Street, Madison, Wisconsin 53703. Copyright © 1978, The Progressive, Inc.

ROSE BOWL SEATS

The Rose Bowl's 104,696 seats would still be half empty if only every adult American who owns $1 million or more in corporate stock came to cheer, and it would be even emptier if only those who have $100,000 in state and local bonds got a seat. If you counted all state, local, and Federal bonds (except U.S. Savings Bonds), and added Treasury bills, certificates, notes, and mortgages — and even foreign bonds — held by Americans in amounts of at least $200,000, you would still find well over a quarter of the Rose Bowl seats not taken. Only 55,400 adults have $1 million or more in corporate stock. A mere 40,000 have $100,000 or more in state and local bonds (all Federal tax exempt), and 73,500 adults have $200,000 or more if we count all bonds and debt-holdings.

This tiny owning class at the tip of the top, barely more than one-twentieth of 1 per cent of American adults, has a fifth of *all* the corporate stock, nearly two-thirds of the worth of *all* state and local bonds, and two-fifths of *all* bonds and notes. No wonder it took five years of trying by an outstanding economist, James D. Smith, to get the IRS to allow him to study its information — and by then some of the data had been destroyed.

Contrast what this propertied class owns to what the rest of us have. Nine out of 10 adults in the United States could sell everything they own, pay off their debts, and have no more than $30,000 left. Worse, more than half of all Americans would have a total "net worth" of no more than $3,000. The bottom half of all American families combined have only three cents of every dollar's worth of all the wealth in the country.

Back at the top, if we count up what the richest one per cent of the population own, we find that they have a seventh of all the real estate in the country, more than half the corporate stock, and almost all the trust assets. They even had a seventh of all the *cash* in every checking and savings account and pocket and purse in America.

Summed up, that is a quarter of the net worth of the entire population held by the top one per cent. If we take a slice as large as the richest four per cent — everyone whose total gross assets (not counting debts) are worth at least $60,000 — their combined wealth is more than a trillion dollars — enough to buy the entire national product of the United States and have plenty left over to pick up the combined output of a few small European countries, including Switzerland, Norway, Denmark, and Sweden.

So it's clear who owns America — but has this propertied class been slipping in its hold on the nation's wealth? Maybe, but if it slipped at all, it was not because of any egalitarian tendencies in American capitalism. It took the country's worst crash, the Great Depression, when many fortunes (and even a few of the fortune-holders) took the plunge from the pinnacle, to make a dent in what they own. Even the modest shrinkage that supposedly took place then is probably more apparent than real, because just before the crash there was a phenomenal rise in the price of stock, the biggest asset in the portfolios of the rich.

But since the end of World War II, there has been no change in their share of the nation's wealth; it has been constant in every year studied, at roughly five-year intervals, since 1945. The richest one per cent own a quarter, and the top half of one per cent a fifth, of the combined market worth of everything owned by every American. Remarkably, economic historians who have culled manuscript census reports on the past century report that on the eve of the Civil War the rich had the same cut of the total: The top one per cent owned 24 per cent in 1860 and 24.9 per cent in 1969 (the latest year thoroughly studied). Through all the tumultuous changes since then — the Civil War and the emancipation of the slaves, the Populist and Progressive movements, the Great Depression, the New Deal, progressive taxation, the mass organization of industrial workers, and World Wars I and II — this class has held on to everything it had. They owned America then and they own it now.

REDISTRIBUTED INCOME?

Any notion that *income* has been redistributed, even though *property* is intact, is also illusory. The higher the income bracket, the higher the percentage in it that derives its income from the ownership of property. At the top, almost all income is in dividends, rents, royalties, and interest. Among all American families and unrelated individuals combined, not more than one in eight receives any stock dividends at all. Not one in 100 receives even a dollar from any "trust or estate." But among those with incomes of $100,000 or more, 97 per cent receive stock dividends and more than half receive inherited income directly from a trust or estate.

The five per cent of Americans with the highest incomes take in almost half of all the income from property in the country. They receive 64 cents out of every dollar in dividends earned on publicly traded stock and 93 cents of the dividends on stock owned in "closely held corporations" (those having just a few owners). Furthermore, they take in 30 cents of every dollar earned in interest, 37 cents in rents and royalties, and 64 cents of every dollar in America coming from trusts and estates.

If we divide Americans into five brackets from low to high, and count all known income, the top fifth gets about 40 cents of every dollar of personal income. The bottom fifth gets just one nickel. That is a ratio of eight to one, and that ratio has remained almost exactly the same in every year since World War II ended. (Here, in the capitalism celebrated by the Advertising Council and Bob Hope, the gap between the top and bottom fifths is wider than in Britain, Holland, West Germany, or even Japan. Among industrial nations, only France has a wider

gap.) And the *real income* gap between the top and bottom has been growing, though the ratio has stayed the same: The average real income difference between the top and bottom fifth, measured in constant 1969 dollars, rose from $11,000 to $19,000 in the 20 years between 1949 and 1969.

All those "redistributive efforts" and wars on poverty we have heard about have not made a dent in income distribution. The overall tax burden has probably become more *regressive* since World War II — taxes are taking an increasing bite of the incomes of people in the lower rather than in the higher brackets. One reason is that state and local taxes, which are typically more regressive than Federal taxes, have grown in comparison to Federal taxes — from 42 cents to every dollar of Federal taxes collected in 1950 to 51 cents in 1961 and 58 cents in 1970.

But even Federal taxes have become more regressive during the same years. Corporate taxes have gone down, from 27 cents of every Federal tax dollar received in 1950 to only 16 cents in 1970, and at the same time Social Security and payroll taxes have jumped from just nine cents to 26 cents of each tax dollar pumped into Washington. So, when the impact of all taxes and all Government spending is taken into account — even though there has been a sizable increase in Government "benefits" to low-income Americans — the level of income inequality ("post-fiscal") has not changed since 1950.

The notion that classes are withering away in America rests not only on the mistaken assumption that the propertied have been lopped off at the top, but on the equally unfounded notion that the working class itself has been vanishing and the "white collar" strata of the so-called middle class have been multiplying. So renowned a pundit as Harvard's John Kenneth Galbraith, among many others, believes the class struggle is a "dwindling phenomenon" because "the number of white-collar workers in the United States almost fifteen years ago overtook the number of the blue-collar working force and is, of course, now greater."

WORKING WOMEN

Of course? The sort of counting done here misses and distorts what has really happened; it confuses occupational composition with class lines. Since the 1900s, especially during World War II, and in quickening pace in recent years, women — and increasingly married women — have been moving into the labor force. About four out of 10 people in the labor force are now women, and almost half of all women now have paying jobs or are looking for them. It is this influx of women into paying jobs that accounts for the growing number of "white-collar" jobs —

mainly in "clerical or sales" work — in the past few decades. Of all working women, not even one in 10 was a "clerical or sales" worker in 1900. By 1940, on the eve of World War II, the figure jumped to almost three in 10, and it climbed until it reached more than four in 10 in 1970.

At the same time, the proportion of women working in crafts or as operatives and laborers (except on the farm) dropped. It also dropped in so-called "service" occupations which, for women, are typically dirty and menial jobs as domestics or "food service" workers. Some "white-collar" jobs are now almost entirely filled by women — and 10 occupations alone, among them waitress, typist, cashier, hairdresser and beautician, nurse and dietician, sales clerk, and teacher, account for more than two out of five employed women. Of all clerical and sales jobs, two out of three, and the same ratio in service jobs, are filled by women. In contrast, of all those working in crafts or as operatives and laborers (off the farm),

only one in six is a woman.

Among men, meanwhile, the portion with clerical and sales jobs has not risen in three decades. Only seven in 100 men at work had clerical or sales jobs in 1900, and it rose to just 12 in 100 by 1940. In the three decades since, the ratio has not grown at all: It is still about 12 in 100. In the same years, though, there has been a significant rise in the proportion of men classified as "professionals and technicians" by the U.S. Census — from three, to six, to 14 in 100. But many such "professionals" are vocational school products, and about four out of 10 in the rapidly-growing category of "technicians" are not college graduates. This, of course, is scarcely the image evoked by the terms "professional" or "technician." Many are really highly-skilled workers; advanced education or certification is not required to fill their jobs, nor does their work differ much in independence and control from the work done by those classified as "craftsmen."

The plain fact is that the category of "manual workers" has not shrunk at all in this century. Fewer than 40 in 100 men worked in 1900 as "craftsman, operative or nonfarm laborer." In 1920, the figure rose to 45 in 100, and it has barely changed since: In 1970, 47 out of every 100 men in the labor force were classified as manual workers. But to this figure we must add many if not most of the men who are called "service workers" — a U.S. Census category that hides a host of blue-collar jobs within its semantic recesses: Janitors, porters, waiters, garage mechanics, dishwashers, and laundry workers. How many of the seven in 100 men in such service jobs in 1970 should be identified as "real workers" is anybody's guess — and mine is that it is most. We must also add an uncounted number of jobs that strangely get catalogued in the Census as "white collar" — among them stock clerks, baggagemen, newspaper carriers ("sales"), and even mailmen. Their work is certainly — and often heavily — "manual labor."

A safe estimate, then, is that more than five of every 10 men who work in this country are manual workers, maybe as many as six in 10 — and this does not count the three out of 100 who work as agricultural laborers. Perhaps the only real difference in the working class today compared to past decades is that many working men now count on their wives' (or daughters') earnings to make the family's ends meet.

In fact, their wives are typically manual workers themselves, for among employed women, the division is sharp between those whose husbands are workers and those who are married to "professionals" or "managers." Among the latter's working wives, only one in six is in manual (or service) jobs. But among the working wives of craftsmen, two in five have such jobs; among the working wives of laborers, about two out of three. They certainly are not smuggling any middle-class values, loyalties, or way of life into the working class based on their own experience at work. For them, on the contrary, as for most men in America, the "yoke of manual labor" is yet to be lifted.

Besides, whatever the social images "manual labor" evokes or whatever pain it involves, in real class terms the distinction between it and "non-manual" or "white-collar" employment is, at best, misleading. How does wearing a white collar lift you into another class? Perhaps there is more prestige attached, though even this is doubtful, particularly among workers themselves. For some "white-collar" workers there may be increased security, but how many cashiers, typists, or beauticians get "salaries" rather than hourly wages, or are less subject to layoffs than highly-organized manual workers?

Since most "white-collar" employees are women, and don't wear collars, white or otherwise, anyway, the name itself surely fools us about what it represents. The vast majority of the clerical and sales workers of today are, in any event, not the respectable clerks of yesteryear. Their work is not only routinized and standardized, but they often work in offices that are larger than (and even as noisy as) small manufacturing shops — tending steno machines, typewriters, accounting machines, data processors, or keypunch equipment. They work in supermarkets and department stores with hundreds of others who punch in and punch out and wait to be relieved before they take a break. They are as bereft of control over their work and the products of their work as "manual" workers — in fact, they have *less* independence and control than such workers as crane operators and longshoremen. Beneath their nice clean collars (if they wear them at all), they are propertyless workers, entirely dependent for their livelihoods on the sale of their capacity to work. And this is the essence of working-class reality.

WHAT 'MANAGERIAL REVOLUTION'?

So, neither the working class nor the propertied class has yet departed our fair land. But do the propertied really make up a *capitalist* class? Haven't they, because ownership of the large corporations has become so dispersed, lost *control* of these decisive units of production in America? Of all the pseudofacts· behind the notion that classes have withered away in America, none is as persistent as the doctrine of the "managerial revolution" or "unseen revolution" implied by these questions.

The claim is that there has been a "separation of ownership and control" in large corporations — that as the corporations have grown immense, as the original founders have died off or their fortunes suppos-

edly dwindled, as their kids have taken to mere coupon-clipping and jet-setting, and as stock ownership has spread out widely, the capitalists have lost control of the means of production. The result, we are told, is that not capital but bureaucracy, not capitalists but "anonymous administrators," now control large corporations and hold decisive power in contemporary America. The "managers" have usurped their capitalist predecessors.

With the capitalists gone and the managers no longer their mere agents, the inherent conflict that used to exist between labor and capital also supposedly becomes a relic of the past. Instead, we now have not a system of class domination but an occupational order based on merit; "rewards" get distributed according to ability ("functional importance"). What's more, with capital dissolved and new managers motivated by other urges and the pride of professionalism in control, pumping out profit is no longer what drives the corporations in the new "post-capitalist society" we are alleged to be living in. Instead, they have become the "trustees," as Prudential's chairman said — and he was just paraphrasing Harvard economist Carl Kaysen's words of 20 years ago — for all of us in the "new industrial state."

The intent of such notions is clear: We are to believe that "labor" and "management" are just parts of the same team, doing different tasks. It is a theoretical shell game that hides the fact of class domination — of the ownership *and* control of the mines, mills, and factories by a class whose lives are certainly made easier if we don't know they're there, right behind the "anonymous bureaucrats." It hides the simple but profound fact that they live on what the rest of us produce.

One reason that the illusion of managerialism persists is that it is incredibly difficult to figure out who does control a large corporation. And the illusion is nurtured, as the late Senator Lee Metcalf put it bluntly and accurately, by a "massive cover-up" of the principal owners. There are several closely related ways that capital really controls the corporations. First, the real owners do not actually have to *manage* the corporation, or hang around the executive suite with its top officers or directors, or even be formally represented on the board, in order to have their objectives realized — that is, to exert *control*. And how much stock it takes to control a corporation is neither fixed nor standard.

The few recent studies that claim to find "management control" in most large corporations simply assume that it always takes at least 10 per cent of the stock in one pair of hands in order to assure control, but it does not work that way. If you own 10 per cent of the stock in a corporation, you are supposed to report it to the Securities and Exchange Commission (SEC), but if the same percentage is split among several of your close associates, without any formal ties between you, or with a few of your relatives, you don't have to report it — and even if you *are* required to report, who is to know if you don't? When Senator Metcalf died, he had been trying for years to get at such information, but his staff so far has had to rely on its own investigations and volunteered data.

How much stock is needed to control a corporation depends on how big the other stockholders are — and who they are, and how they are connected — and how dispersed the rest of the stock is; it also depends on how deeply the firm is indebted to the same few large banks or other creditors. What sorts of ties the corporation has to others, and especially to big banks and other "financial institutions" allied with it, is also crucial. The ability to exert control grows with the number of other major firms in which any family, individual, or group of associates has an interest or actual control.

FAMILY HOLDINGS

What a particular large holding of stock implies for any attempt at control depends to an unknown extent on who holds it. If it is held, say, by a leading capitalist family like the Mellons — who control at least four firms in the top 500 nonfinancials (Gulf, Alcoa, Koppers Co., Carborundum Co.) as well as the First Boston Corp., the General Reinsurance Corp., and Mellon National Bank and Trust (the 15th largest bank in the country, measured by deposits), and perhaps also, through the Mellon Bank's per cent on shareholding, Jones and Laughlin Steel — the meaning is just not the same as if some otherwise unconnected shareowner held it.

Even in corporations that a family like Mellon does not control, the presence of its representative among the principal shareowners, or on the board, can be critical. So the late Richard King Mellon, as one of the principal shareowners in General Motors, carried a rather different clout in its corporate policy than,

say, Billy Rose did in AT&T, though he was reputed to be one of its biggest shareowners. Precisely because the number of shareowners is so large and their holdings typically so minute compared to the few biggest shareowners in a large corporation, it may not take more than 1 or 2 per cent of a company's stock to control it.

The critical holdings and connections that make control possible are invisible to the uninformed eye, and often even to the seasoned investigator. Senator Metcalf's staff found, for instance, that Laurance S. Rockefeller owns a controlling block of almost 5 per cent of the voting stock in Eastern Airlines, though his name did not appear on the required listing of its 30 top stockholders for the Civil Aeronautics Board. Neither the SEC nor the CAB nor Eastern itself could find all the accounts in which his shares were held and aggregate them until they asked *him* to do it for them — in response to Metcalf's prodding.

This helps explain why even the "insiders" who work as financial analysts at *Fortune*, *Forbes*, or *Business Week*, with their immense research resources and excellent files, have to rely heavily on gossip to estimate the holdings of even the leading families in corporations they have long controlled. These holdings are hidden in a welter of accounts held by brokers, dealers, foundations, holding companies, other corporations, associates, intermediaries, and "street names" (as fictitious firms that just hold stock for someone are called on Wall Street) or other "nominees."

The extent of a leading capitalist family's holdings is also concealed by a finely woven though tangled web of kinship relations. Apparently unrelated persons with entirely different surnames can be part of a single cohesive set of kindred united to control a corporation. In Dow Chemical Company, for instance, there are 78 dependents (plus spouses) of H. W. Dow who own a total of 12.6 per cent of Dow's stock. So, without research aimed at penetrating the web of kinship, any effort to find out who really controls a large corporation is hobbled at the outset.

In an outstanding recent study, Philip Burch Jr. mined the "inside information" presented over the years in the financial press and found that at least 60 per cent of the 500 top industrial corporations are "probably" (236) or "possibly" (64) under the control of an identifiable family or group of associates. Even these estimates are probably short of the mark because, in Ralph Nader's words, "no one really knows who owns the giant corporations that dominate our economic life." My own guess is that behind the thick veil of nominees, there are real controlling owners in most if not all of the large corporations that now appear to be under so-called management control.

Even if some large corporations were not really controlled by *particular* owning interests, this would not mean power had passed to the "new princes" from the old economic royalists. The higher executives would still have only *relative* independence in their activities and would be bound by the *general* interests of capital. The heads of the large corporations are the main formal agents or functionaries of capital. Their personal careers, interests, and commitments are closely tied to the expansion of corporate capital. Some are among the principal shareholders of the companies they run, and most own stock that not only provides much of their income but ranks them among the population's largest stockowners — and puts them in the propertied few.

Typically, the managers also move in the same intimate circles as the very rich. You'll find them together at debutante balls, select clubs, summer resorts and winter retreats, and other assorted watering places; and their kids attend the same private schools and rush the same fraternities and sororities — and then marry each other. Scratch a top executive and the chances are he will prove to be related to a principal shareowner. Intimate social ties and entangling kinship relations, common interests and overriding commitments unify the families of the heads of the largest corporations and their principal owners into the same cohesive, dominant class in America.

Finally, even if "management" alone had full control of the corporations, it would still have to try to pump the highest possible profits out of their workers and make the most of their investments. The conduct of management is shaped above all by the imperatives of capital accumulation — the competitive struggle among the giants (now global rather than national), the types of investments they make and markets they penetrate, and the relations they have with their workers. High managerial income and status depend, directly and indirectly, on high corporate profits. "Stock options" and bonuses and other forms of executive "compensation" aside from salaries are closely tied to corporate profit rates.

Whatever their so-called professional motivations or power urges, their technocratic teamwork and bureaucratic mentality, managers' decisions on how to organize production and sales have to be measured against the bottom line. They dare not imperil corporate profitability.

The recent spate of articles in the financial press on "how to fire a top executive" — you have them "take early retirement" — and the new placement services now catering to them, are rather pointed indicators of what happens to supposed "management control" in times of receding profit margins. In 1974, a year of severe economic crisis around the world, about half of all the chief executives in the nation's top 500 firms were expected to be replaced — in what a weekly newsletter to corporate heads called "a wave of executive ousters" that would "cause the greatest disruption in the business community since the 1929 depression."

Any obvious lowering in profit rates is also reflected in a drop in the price of the corporation's stock; this squeezes its capital base and makes it an attractive — and vulnerable — target for takeover. And this, in turn, leads to executive ousters. In addition, with the marked centralization of huge shareholdings in the trust departments of a few of the biggest banks that administer the investment portfolios of the very rich — typically, they will not take a trust of under $200,000 — the tremors would be deep and the impact rather painful for any managers who turned out a below-average rate of return. The banks must unflinchingly act as "trustees" only for the top investors and real owners who control the large corporations.

Any political strategy that ignores or distorts these realities or is blind to the deep class divisions in our country cannot meet the common needs of the majority of Americans. So long as the illusion persists that our economic life has been "democratized" or that a "silent revolution" has already interred capital, emancipated labor, and redistributed wealth and income, we can be sure that a real effort to achieve those aims will be slated for yet another postponement. ■

Private Anger and Public Protest

by Frances Fox Piven

The bottom line of U.S. urban economic policies today is to be found in the actual, tangible experiences of our inner city poor. The bottom line has to do with the persistence of unemployment, so enduring as to deprive the poor of their physical and psychological capacities for work and for normal life. The bottom line has to do with the utter collapse of the low rental housing market with the result that whole neighborhoods have been reduced to rubble. And under these circumstances the *communities* of the poor collapse, so that whatever they have in the way of infrastructure or a capacity for self-help is gone.

At the same time, and as a result of the so-called fiscal crisis, whatever neighborhood services the older cities once provided for the casualties of our economic policies have been cut back. The paltry services, the centers for senior citizens, the drug programs — all these are going. With the opportunity to work and to live a normal life denied, the people of the inner city are forging an alternative culture of their own. It is a culture built on despair — a culture of social suicide, a culture of drugs and a culture of crime, which leads many of us, of course, to castigate and to scapegoat them even more. In short, the bottom line of our economic and social policies is the destruction of the urban lower class in the United States today, and there is no more moderate way of stating it. We are destroying the lower stratum of our population.

The puzzle is that in American political principle none of this should be happening. During the 1960s we experienced what might be called the blossoming of reform and of plans to implement these reforms. We generated good ideas about how our government could act to secure a more human kind of life for people at the bottom of American society.

The second puzzle is that the toll has been most catastrophic on inner city blacks. In the 1960s, black

Dr. Frances Fox Piven is professor of political science, Boston University. The article above is excerpted from her talk before a Joint Session of the Urban Bishops' Coalition and the Church and City Conference. It was first printed in THE WITNESS magazine, January 1979.

people won an impressive victory. They won the right to vote in the South and the right to representation in the North. But in the wake of the grand promises attached to the franchise, the circumstances of the black, urban poor are worsening.

The reason for these failures is that great profits are made through existing economic policies and therefore, there is powerful resistance to change. In the face of that power, the right to vote is a very weak weapon, indeed. Throughout American history, gains have never been made by poor people simply through propounding good ideas. Rather, gains by people who are at the bottom of American society have been won only through mass protests, through large scale defiance and as a result of subsequent institutional and political reverberations.

If that sounds like an outrageous statement, let me suggest some evidence for it. In 1933 the poor in the United States won for the first time a national relief policy which provided for the unemployed a minimum of subsistence in the face of economic catastrophe. It was a victory won only over powerful resistance. How then was it won? In the early 1930s, the unemployed themselves somehow found the courage to make trouble in the cities in which they were concentrated. They engaged in actions called rent riots in which they gathered together and resisted the marshal and refused to be evicted. They engaged in relief riots, taking over private relief agencies or local relief agencies which gave out coal and food baskets. The institutional impact of this movement of the unemployed was severe. In city after city mayors and local businesses were confronted on the one hand with an insurgent unemployed population and on the other with a circumstance we know now as fiscal crisis. So that in 1933, in the wake of a dramatic electoral turnabout, Franklin D. Roosevelt, in the space of 45 days, initiated the first major national relief program in American history.

Another victory won in the 1930s was the right of industrial workers to organize. That also was over the opposition of industrialists who had commandeered the courts, the government, their own private police, and the whole community propaganda apparatus in which industries were located. Industry was determined that workers not organize. But in the face of the depression, wage cuts, and with the inspiration created by a New Deal in Washington, workers began to walk out in large numbers; to sit down in factories; to organize their self-defense against the company police and the militia who had in American history always destroyed strikes. And in the face of that massive movement of militant protesting workers, FDR put his support behind the Wagner Act and later behind the "Wages and Hours Act." He then appointed pro labor representatives to the new NLRB. And this was all won by industrial workers through massive protest.

Examples abound from more recent times. In the late 1950s and 1960s black people in the South mounted a massive protest movement. These were people who had been displaced by the mechanization of plantations, a labor intensive form of agriculture that threw out the day laborers, sharecroppers, and farmers it no longer needed. And many of these people migrated to the Southern cities. There they began to demand some of the Civil Rights other Americans had been enjoying. They found the solidarity first to boycott on a massive scale and then later, beginning in Albany, to fill the jails on a massive scale. They found the courage to engage in freedom riots and marches. And they were helped to find that courage in the late 1950s and the 1960s by their churches.

Finally, black people were offered concessions which had to do with Civil Rights and ultimately with the elimination of terror from the arsenal of political controls over blacks in the South. Black people did win the franchise, but only through a vigorous protest movement.

The moral of the actual history of struggles of people at the bottom of American society is very different from the civics lessons we are wont to preach. It is that poor people and working people sometimes do win, but only through protest. They win only when they find the courage to defy the institutional rules and the authorities which ordinarily keep them quiescent. They win only when they create sufficient trouble in the institutions of American society, so as to make political leaders worry.

Today, the inner city poor are quiet. And the economic policies which have generated their poverty and their destruction are moving forward unfettered. Many of the gains that were won in the 1960s are being reversed, and the disintegration of life at the bottom is accelerated. If the process is to be halted it can only be through the development of mass protests comparable in extent to those that won earlier concessions.

What role then will the churches play in all of this? The churches provide much of the moral leadership and the community leadership in poor and working class communities. How that role is acted out makes a difference one way or the other. Through most of our history, churches have used the transforming power of the gospel to transform low income working people into quiescence. Through most of our history, our churches have used their capacity for leadership to teach people to accept state authority and economic authority, and to look for salvation in another life. But sometimes the Church has played a different role. It is worth looking backward at what some church leaders did both in the Civil Rights movement and in the ghetto movement, and what the Roman Catholic Church is now doing in Latin America and even in our cities today.

The very fact that churches provide moral leadership to a community means they are virtually determining whether the poor and working people think that the grievances, the sufferings which they experience are justified or unjustified; whether they are inevitable or can be changed. That moral role — the capacity to help people turn private anger into public indignation — is crucial. Also, churches through their moral authority can help people to define the ingrained prohibitions which deter people from making demands, from asserting rights.

Moreover, the churches are in a position to help promote and to facilitate collective defiance and to do that not only by lending moral authority to rent strikes, to the demands of welfare recipients, to the school boycotts and to demonstrations over employment; but also by lending the physical facilities to those protest movements that do emerge. That also was done during the Civil Rights movement of the '30s and '60s, and in the ghetto movement in the late '60s. This is not to say that the churches made those movements emerge. Movements of low income and working people in the United States emerge from forces far larger than even churches can command. What is important is that as in the recent past, churches not restrain those movements but rather, encourage them.

Now, it is also true that the Church can do many other things and do them usefully. The Church can make recommendations to the American ruling class about how to reorganize the economy. The Church can work out policy positions, detailed plans about how that organization ought to proceed. But I propose that the transforming power of the gospel in the United States today is not likely to achieve its greatest effects in its attempts to transform the wealthy. Rather, the transforming power of the gospel, if it is truly to be a nourishing and vigorous force, ought to orient itself to the poor, to the working people who are the victims of wealth and power. And there comes a time when a truly religious mission is a political mission as well. ∎

Christian Solidarity and Class Struggle

by Gustavo Gutierrez

Human solidarity, which has as its ultimate basis our brotherhood and sisterhood before God, is built in history. Today history is characterized by conflict which seems to impede this building of unity. There is one characteristic in particular which holds a central place: The division of humanity into oppressors and oppressed, into owners of the means of production and those dispossessed of the fruit of their work, into antagonistic social classes. But this is not all; the division brings with it confrontations, struggles, violence. How then are we to live evangelical charity in the midst of this situation? How can we reconcile the universality of charity with the option for a particular social class? Unity is one of the notes of the Church and yet the class struggle divides people; is the unity of the Church compatible with class struggle? . . .

. . .The class struggle is one of the cardinal problems of the world today which challenges the life and reflection of the Christian community and which can no longer be avoided. It is undeniable that the class struggle poses problems to the universality of Christian love and the unity of the Church. But any consideration of this subject must start from two elemental points: The class struggle is a fact, and neutrality in this matter is impossible.

THE CLASS STRUGGLE

The class struggle is a part of our economic, social, political, cultural, and religious reality. Its evolution, its exact extent, its nuances, and its variations are the object of analysis of the social sciences and pertain to the field of scientific rationality.

Recognition of the existence of the class struggle does not depend on our religious or ethical options.

Gustavo Gutierrez is a theologian and professor of theology at the Catholic University in Lima, Peru. The above article was excerpted from *A Theology of Liberation*, Copyright © by Orbis Books, Maryknoll, N.Y., 10545. Reprinted by permission.

There are those who have claimed that it is something artificial, foreign to the norms which guide our society, contrary to the spirit of "Western Christian civilization," and the work of agitators and malcontents. Perhaps in spite of those who think this way, there is one thing that is true in this viewpoint: Oppression and exploitation, and therefore the experience of the class struggle, are endured and perceived first of all by those who have been marginated by that civilization and do not have their own voice in the Church. Although there is an awareness of the class struggle on the periphery, this does not mean that the struggle does not exist at the center of society: The dispossessed exist because of those who direct and govern this society. The class struggle is the product of demented minds only for those who do not know, or who do not wish to know, what is produced by the system. As the French bishops stated some years ago, "The class struggle is first of all a fact which no one can deny." And they continue, "At the level of those responsible for the class struggle, the first are those who voluntarily keep the working class in an unjust situation, who oppose their collective advancement, and combat their efforts to liberate themselves."

Those who speak of class struggle do not "advocate" it — as some would say — in the sense of creating it out of nothing by an act of (bad) will. What they do is to recognize a fact and contribute to an awareness of that fact. And there is nothing more certain than a fact. To ignore it is to deceive and to be deceived and moreover to deprive oneself of the necessary means of truly and radically eliminating this condition — that is, by moving toward a classless society. Paradoxically, what the groups in power call "advocating" class struggle is really an expression of a will to abolish its causes, to abolish them, not cover them over, to eliminate the appropriation by a few of the wealth created by the work of the many and not to make lyrical calls to social harmony. It is a will to build a socialist society, more just, free, and human, and not a society of superficial and false reconciliation and equality. To "advocate" class struggle, therefore, is to reject a situation in which there are oppressed and oppressors. But it is a rejection without deceit or cowardliness; it is to recognize that the fact exists and that it profoundly divides people, in order to be able to attack it at its roots and thus create the conditions of an authentic human community. To build a just society today necessarily implies the active and conscious participation in the class struggle that is occurring before our eyes.

NEUTRALITY IMPOSSIBLE

In the second place, we must see clearly that to deny the fact of class struggle is really to put oneself on the side of the dominant sectors. Neutrality is impossible. It is not a question of admitting or denying a fact which confronts us; rather it is a question of which side we are on. . . . When the Church rejects the class struggle, it is objectively operating as a part of the prevailing system. By denying the existence of social division, this system seeks to perpetuate this division on which are based the privileges of its beneficiaries. It is a classist option, deceitfully camouflaged by a purported equality before the law. The history of this refusal is long, and its causes many and complex. But the ever more acute awareness that the oppressed have of their situation and the increasing participation of Christians in the class struggle are raising new questions in the Church which are more authentic and real.

The class struggle is a fact and neutrality in this question is not possible. These two observations delimit the indicated problems, prevent us from getting lost in facile solutions, and provide a concrete context for our search. More exactly, the questions raised with regard to the universal character of love and the unity of the Church are real questions precisely because the class struggle confronts us as a fact and because it is impossible not to take part in it.

The gospel announces the love of God for all people and calls us to love as God loves. But to accept class struggle means to decide for some people and against others. To live both realities without juxtapositions is a great challenge for the Christian committed to the totality of the process of liberation. This is a challenge that leads us to deepen our faith and to mature in our love for others.

The universality of Christian love is only an abstraction unless it becomes concrete history, process, conflict; it is arrived at only through particularity. To love all people does not mean avoiding confrontations; it does not mean preserving a fictitious harmony. Universal love is that which in solidarity with the oppressed seeks also to liberate

i was hungry and
you blamed it on the
communists
i was hungry and you
circled the moon
i was hungry and you
told me to wait
i was hungry and you said
"so were my ancestors"
i was hungry and you said,
we don't hire over 35
i was hungry and you said,
God helps those . . .
i was hungry and you told me
i shouldn't be
i was hungry and you told me
machines do that work now
i was hungry and you
had napalm bills
to pay
i was hungry and you said,
the poor are always with us.
Lord,
when did we see you hungry?
Matthew 25:37

the oppressors from their own power, from their ambition, and from their selfishness: "Love for those who live in a condition of objective sin demands that we struggle to liberate them from it. The liberation of the poor and the liberation of the rich are achieved simultaneously." One loves the oppressors by liberating them from their inhuman condition as oppressors, by liberating them from themselves. But this cannot be achieved except by resolutely opting for the oppressed, that is, by combatting the oppressive class. It must be a real and effective combat, not hate. This is the challenge, as new as the gospel: To love our enemies. This was never thought to be easy, but as long as it was only a question of showing a certain sweetness of character, it was preached without difficulty. The counsel was not followed, but it was heard without any uneasiness. In the context of class struggle today, to love one's enemies presupposes recognizing and accepting that one has class enemies and that it is necessary to combat them. It is not a question of having no enemies, but rather of not excluding them from our love. But love does not mean that the oppressors are no longer enemies, nor does it eliminate the radicalness of the combat against them. "Love of enemies" does not ease tensions; rather it challenges the whole system and becomes a subversive formula.

Universal love comes down from the level of abstractions and becomes concrete and effective by becoming incarnate in the struggle for the liberation of the oppressed. It is a question of loving all people, not in some vague, general way, but rather in exploited persons, in concrete persons who are struggling to live humanly. Our love for them does not "abstract" them, it does not isolate them from the social class to which they belong, so that we can have "pity" on them. On the contrary, our love is not authentic if it does not take the path of class solidarity and social struggle. To participate in class struggle not only is not opposed to universal love; this commitment is today the necessary and inescapable means of making this love concrete. For this participation is what leads to a classless society without owners and dispossessed, without oppressors and oppressed. In dialectical thinking, reconciliation is the overcoming of conflict. The communion of paschal joy passes through confrontation and the cross.

The fact of class struggle also challenges the unity of the Church and demands a redefinition of what we understand by this unity.

The Church is in a world divided into antagonistic social classes, on a universal scale as well as at the local level. Because it is present in our society, the Church cannot attempt to ignore a fact which confronts it. What is more, this fact exists within the Church itself. Indeed, Christians belong to opposing social classes, which means that the Christian community itself is split by this social division. It is not possible to speak of the unity of the Church without taking into account its concrete situation in the world.

To try piously to cover over this social division with a fictitious and formalistic unity is to avoid a difficult and conflictual reality and definitely to join the dominant class. It is to falsify the true character of the Christian community under the pretext of a religious attitude which tries to place itself beyond temporal contingencies. In these conditions, to speak, for example, of the priest as "the symbol of unity" is to attempt to make the priest into a part of

the prevailing system. It is to attempt to make the priest a part of an unjust and oppressive system, based on the exploitation of the great majorities and needing a religious justification to preserve itself. This is especially true in places like Latin America, where the Church has a great influence among the exploited masses. . . .

In a radically divided world, the function of the ecclesial community is to struggle against the profound causes of the division among people. . . . For the ecclesial community to recognize the fact of class struggle and to participate actively in it will not be therefore a negation of the message of unity which it bears; rather it will be to discover the path by which it can free itself from that which now prevents it from being a clear and true sign of brotherhood and sisterhood.

This perspective is, among other things, changing the focus of the concerns of ecumenism. Christians of different confessions are taking similar positions regarding the misery and injustice in Latin America, and this unites them more strongly than intraecclesial considerations. Christian unity thus begins to present questions very different than those we receive from Europe. Because of a more realistic focus for its presence in the world and its commitment to the disinherited, Christians in Latin America are united and divided in ways and for reasons very different than in past years. The paths which lead to accepting the gift of unity in Christ and His Spirit in history are going through unecclesiastical places. A new kind of ecumenism is being born.

If the historical and social coordinates of the Christian community are not taken into account, any reflection will not be critical or sound and will serve only to preserve the status quo and justify attitudes which evade reality. On the other hand, if we start from the concrete realities of the presence of the Church in a society which is divided and conflictual and which at the same time is engaged in creating a more human world, then we might be able to indicate new directions for ecclesiology. ∎

Group Exercise

A booklet entitled, *The Corporate Captivity of the Church* points out that Christians have been called to be "in the world but not of it," yet the churches have not seriously challenged corporatist values. U.S. Church assets total $134.3 billion, which includes real estate, business, cemeteries, camps, church and school buildings, stocks and bonds. And each year the cash flow through Christian religious institutions amounts to $21 billion.

The booklet goes on to say that a corporatist ethos pervades church board meetings and the vision of the church is relegated to "goals and objectives" and rules of "proper management." Financial and investment committees make their decisions along the lines of highest profitability and the rule of Wall Street.

This exercise is designed to help us look at some of the hard systemic questions that Christians face surrounding investments. Using *ROLE PLAY* we will try to examine some of the various positions of key persons who support this close connection between the business world and the churches, and the growing number of persons who oppose such a close relationship. The prophetic Church challenges Christian commitment to a system based on competition and profits which creates much of the exploitation that we have seen in previous weeks' readings.

The scene is this: Some of you will be asked to serve on a public panel designed to explore the issues surrounding church investments in global corporations. Others will be members of the audience and will need to be prepared to ask questions of the panelists.

The panel is comprised of:

1 Bishop: Whose diocese/district has more than $3 million invested in the corporations described below. He is socially concerned, but is also concerned about maintaining financial accountability for his church's assets.

2 Bank President: Who comes to defend his bank's decision to invest in the corporations described below. He has also served as financial officer in counseling the diocese to invest in the same corporations.

3 Pastor/Priest: Who has worked with the Social Action Committee which called this public panel. S/he recognizes the bind the Bishop and church are in, but is also aware of the call of the gospel to serve the poor and oppressed. S/he has become increasingly aware of the role of U.S. corporate penetration of the Third World as well as its domestic impact.

4 Chairperson of Social Action Committee: Whose committee has initiated this public panel to discuss church investments in global corporations. The committee has spent one year studying the impact of investments abroad and at home and is now recommending that the church withdraw all funds from the corporations described below and that the money be used to set up a program to serve the interest of the poor and exploited in this Mid-western industrial town, where unemployment is high (particularly among national minorities, women, and young people).

These are the four corporations that are being challenged. Implicit in this challenge is the entire concept of church monies being used to support a system based on the right to private ownership of social wealth and motivated by the pursuit of profit which creates an international system of exploitation.

1) Nestle's produces and markets infant formula around the world. You recall from a recent missionary's visit that the use of infant formulas in Third World countries is a problem because in many instances, poor water supplies and lack of refrigeration make it dangerous. Poor families also are unable to pay for the increasing amounts of formula needed by growing children. You recall that many corporations are responsible for marketing products in such a way that consumers are frequently unaware of the potential hazards.

2) Gulf & Western is developing agribusiness in the Dominican Republic. Many small farms are going out of business and land is being accumulated by a few owners. An increasing number of farm workers are left without the means of making a living. Crops that are produced on Gulf & Western's large estates are exported to feed First World countries, while many Dominicans go hungry.

3) Federal Mogul, a roller bearing producer for the auto industry, has moved large productive facilities from the North to the South. It has left 2,000 workers unemployed in Detroit. A diminishing tax base and rising unemployment have created severe social problems. Meanwhile, the company has moved to Alabama, a "right-to-work" state, where labor is less organized and workers can be hired for lower wages. Poor benefits, long work days and no job security have become hallmarks of this company.

4) IBM, an "Equal Opportunity Employer," continues to do business in apartheid South Africa. IBM refuses to divest because, it argues, "We are giving jobs to blacks."

PROCESS FOR EXERCISE: Begin by dividing your group into four sections. Group One is the support group for the Bishop; Group Two, the Bank President; Group Three, the Pastor/Priest; and Group Four, the

Chairperson. Each group will take 10 minutes to elect their representative for the panel and to develop arguments consonant with the roles described above.

The four panelists take their place and each member will take three minutes to present his/her argument on the question: "Church investments in global corporations: A help or a hindrance for social justice?"

At the end of the presentations, allow five minutes for questions among the panelists, and then allow for 15 minutes of discussion and questions with the other group members, representing the audience at this public hearing.

Use the final 15 minutes of this hour role playing session to debrief the game, noting down on newsprint some of the questions raised. What contradictions did the panelists and the audience surface between business and gospel? Did your group believe it was possible to improve the arrangement of financial investments, or did your group note an inherent contradiction between advocating social justice while maintaining investments in profit making corporations? What other issues were raised by your group?

For the remaining hour of the session, discuss the questions below:

1 In what kinds of companies do our denominations invest their monies? How are the monies of our church pension funds invested? (Your group might want to discuss setting up a committee to investigate these areas.) Is it merely a question of seeking better companies, or is there something larger at stake than the moral question as we discuss the investment strategies?

Luke 4:16-22: He came to Nazareth, where he had been brought up, and went into the synagogue on the sabbath day as he usually did. He stood up to read, and they handed him the scroll of the prophet Isaiah. Unrolling the scroll, he found the place where it is written: "The spirit of the Lord has been given to me/ for he has anointed me./ He has sent me to bring the good news to the poor/ to proclaim liberty to captives/ and to the blind new sight/ to set the downtrodden free/ to proclaim the Lord's year of favor." He then rolled up the scroll, gave it back to the assistant and sat down. And all eyes in the synagogue were fixed on him. Then he began to speak to them, "This text is being fulfilled today even as you listen."

2 Does our understanding of God and the mission of Jesus give us any clues when faced with the contradiction of seeking profit through corporate investment and identifying with working people and the poor? What insights does Luke 4:16-22 offer? What was the choice that Jesus made? Whose side was He on?

3 Theologians and religious leaders of the Third World are saying that to be Christian today means we must identify with the poor. What are some ways in which we can do that? What would it mean for us to begin resisting oppression in a systemic way? Whose interests do our church investment programs serve? Which class is likely to benefit most? What are some ways we can begin to relate our faith to working class consciousness; to the poor and excluded?

4 Frequently people who live in the United States think of Marxism in terms such as *totalitarian, atheistic,* or as ''a subversive theory which preaches violence and terrorism.'' What was your concept of Marxism before reading the selections by Frank Cunningham? Has your impression changed? Have you read the *Communist Manifesto* or other classical works by Marx, Engels, Lenin? If so, why? If not, why not? Is there such a thing as *atheistic capitalism*?

5 Frances Fox Piven suggests a number of ways the churches can be advocates for the poor and can be involved in the struggle of working people to overcome their exploitation. Can you suggest other ways in which your parish can become involved in liberation efforts? What concrete steps can be taken to manifest your congregation's option for the poor? Is there a theological tradition for such a choice?

Reclaiming Our Christian Tradition

By this time we are all well aware of the considerable difference between the focus of this study guide and the concerns of most of the churches of which we have been a part. For example, the subject of class and economic injustice is almost universally ignored by churches. Our reaction could be a sense of betrayal: "Why haven't these concerns been evident in churches all along?" Or it may be one of suspicion: "Are Gustavo Gutierrez and Sheila Collins really speaking in the spirit of the authentic gospel? If so, why has this kind of perspective been so muted in our experience?"

The gap between the gospel mandate as presented in this study and the Christian faith as taught to us in our previous education has its origins in Fourth Century A.D., when Emperor Constantine adopted Christianity not only as his personal faith, but as the official religion of the empire. Replacing the Greco-Roman religion, Christianity was made the spiritual cement for an imperial domain. This was a role basically incompatible with its origin among the dispossessed and its faith that in Christ, God "has put down the mighty from their thrones and exalted those of low degree" (Luke 1:52).

Ever since Constantine, Christianity has been the official religion of the West, whether formally through established state churches, such as the Church of England, or informally as in the United States. The reigning political and social forces have fought continuously to prevent the Christian faith from threatening the established way of doing things and to use Christianity as the justification for the *status quo*. In the Middle Ages, Christianity served to justify feudalism; then when capitalism replaced feudalism, Christianity, especially in its Protestant form, served to sanctify the capitalist economic order. We are all familiar with how Christianity has been used as justification for waging wars, taking colonies or instituting slavery and apartheid. Even Adolf Hitler successfully reshaped a large portion of the German Church to fit his racist imperialism.

By and large, Christianity has been shaped by the perceived needs of the prevailing power structure to justify the existing distribution of power. In the United States, and in the West in general, most of the power of the Christian faith to raise uncomfortable questions about economic justice, class divisions, racism, sexism and imperialism has been lost through individualizing and spiritualizing the Christian faith.

For most of us, faith has been reduced to a basically individual matter between us and God, with ramifications extending probably not far beyond questions of individual morality among family, friends and co-workers.

At these points where the gospel unmistakably addresses economic injustice and human oppression, the passages are spiritualized. Thus, Jesus' announcement of His own ministry to bring "good news to the poor" and "to liberate the oppressed" (Luke 4:18-22) is interpreted to apply just to the spiritually poor and the spiritually oppressed.

But in spite of all the forces which have sought to domesticate the gospel, its power to address injustice has broken through at many points in Christian history. The earliest Christian communities were persecuted for proclaiming that "Jesus Christ is Lord" *not* Caesar. In the 13th Century, Francis of Assisi founded an association of imitators of Christ, practicing a life of poverty and caring for lepers and outcasts. In the 16th Century, a group of Anabaptists formed the Hutterite Brethren and gave up private property in favor of the common sharing of all property. More recently, this impulse has been embodied by Dorothy Day and Peter Maurin, who in 1933 founded the Catholic Worker movement to minister among the poor.

Frequently the power of the gospel to bring justice has broken out most dramatically in ways that directly challenge the established churches. When the Nazis sought to bring German Protestantism under their sway, the

German "Confessing Church" (including Dietrich Bonhoeffer and Karl Barth) arose to demand that their church be the *Church*, not an adjunct to Nazism. When the Protestant Episcopal Church in the U.S. continued to drag its feet in ordaining women, four bishops ordained 11 women in 1974 in defiance of church law, paving the way for the eventual dropping of barriers against women priests.

Often it has been oppressed groups who have led the way, recognizing in the gospel the special compassion of God for the oppressed. Black Christians in the United States, for instance, have been a deeply religious people and their spirituality has carried both an earthly and transcendent meaning. "Comin' for to carry me home" means the hope of liberation from human bondage as well as a spiritual freedom. Much of the churches' present concern for justice derives from the leadership of Martin Luther King, Jr. and the black churches in the civil rights movement, beginning with the 1956 bus boycott in Montgomery, Alabama.

In our day we are witnessing a significant rebellion by oppressed people and their allies against the age-old distortions of the Christian faith. Sheila Collins' article, "Reclaiming the Bible through Story-telling" is an example of the perspective taken by a highly-energized group of women theologians in the United States. Gustavo Gutierrez, whose "Christian Solidarity and Class Struggle" was read in Session Four, is a leader among the pathbreaking group of Latin American liberation theologians, who now have their counterparts in every area of the Third World. Similar work is being done by Native Americans, Asian-Americans, Afro-Americans, and Hispanic Americans.

In this session we shall examine the way in which the Christian tradition is being reclaimed on behalf of the liberating struggle by three major groups of Christians in the U.S. — black, Hispanic, and a group of predominantly white Christians.

These new perspectives — though in another sense they are really "the old, old story" — also find their expression in a different kind of worship and biblical interpretation which avoids individualism and spiritualization. An example offered in this session is the interpretation of the first chapters of Exodus by Pablo Richard, an exiled Chilean layman immersed in the liberation struggles of Latin America. ∎

Reclaiming the Bible Through Storytelling

by Sheila Collins

When I attended seminary, theology began deductively, with abstract syllogisms composed by men, usually with German names — men who had never had to change and wash dirty diapers, sit for six hours in the welfare office, stay up all night with a sick child, pick cotton in a dusty field, sell their bodies for a living, or work all day in the mills and then come home to do the dinner, the laundry, and the dishes.

Such men had wives and secretaries to take care of their bodily needs. Their sons and daughters went to Harvard and Oberlin (or their German equivalents), not to Pleiku or the Scotia mine pits. They were paid handsomely to spin out beautiful theories which only their peers could understand. They claimed that their theories were derived from the Bible, and it took them hundreds of pages to explain why. I believe it took them hundreds of pages because their process was inherently unbiblical.

If theology is to be meaningful for us, it must not start with abstractions, but with *our stories* — just as the early Hebrews and Christians of the Bible began with theirs. Somehow, our churches got the order reversed. How many of us were taught as children to memorize Bible stories and verses before we ever understood or had a chance to articulate our own story? We cannot appreciate the meaning of another's experience — especially if that experience occurred two and three thousand years ago — until we have asked the right questions of our own.

I see the Bible, not as a set of facts or propositions to which we must twist experience to fit, but as a guide or primer to participating in the creation of our own biblical history. The mistake (or perhaps the deliberate tactic) of the official Christian church was to make us believe that biblical history stopped at the end of the First Century A.D., just as our schools

Sheila Collins is with the National Division of the Board of Global Ministries of the United Methodist Church. The above is excerpted from Document #3 of a series distributed by the Secretariat of Theology in the Americas in New York, and is the result of Ms. Collins' work with the TIA Women's Project, "Women, Work and the Economy." It first appeared in THE WITNESS magazine, September, 1978.

have taught us that American history began with Columbus or the Mayflower. To the extent that those of us who call ourselves Christian still find important the cluster of meanings surrounding the Exodus, the entry into the Promised Land, the ministry, death and resurrection of Jesus, we participate in shaping the continuation of that story, just as surely as did Moses and Miriam, Peter, Priscilla and Paul.

Theology begins with our stories: What we do with our time; how we feel about our children, our husbands, our bosses; how we feel about money and who gets it; what we do when we get up in the morning; how we make it through the day; what pains us, enrages us, saddens and humiliates us; what makes us laugh; what enlightens and empowers us; what keeps us holding on in moments of despair; where we find separation and alienation; where we find true community and trust.

When I say that theology starts with our stories I am not saying anything new. Testifying is a cherished tradition and telling our stories to one another is what women have always done — over the garden fence, at the food co-op, down at the pump. The tradition is the same, only the structure and significance we give to it are different.

Testifying in church usually signifies you've already been saved. One isn't suppposed to talk about troubles unless one's already found Jesus and arrived in the Promised Land. But if you're still in the wilderness, it's pretty hard to see your way through. And if you're still in bondage back in Egypt, you might not even know there is a liberator who has just been found among the bullrushes. Yet if the Hebrews had not preserved the stories as they went along — stories of groaning and complaining; stories of despair — if they had had no rich oral tradition to preserve the sting of the lash, the memory of having sown while another reaped, how would they have known what the taste of liberation was all about? How would they have recognized it when it came?

Our churches, promulgating a pietism which is false to the continuous reversals of our experience and to the experience of those in the Bible, have not offered us women a place to speak our bitterness. And if we have not been able to name our pain to see the collective parameters of our oppression, how shall we be able to name the Kingdom which lies past our suffering except as that "Jubilee Land" to which we return beyond the veil of death?

By telling our stories we must force our churches to hear what we have suffered and the ways in which we have gotten through. We must pull them away from their domesticity and otherworldly preoccupations and force them to deal with the nitty gritty of bread and justice. But we cannot tell our stories as we have done in the past — as an endless litany of individual disasters and unimportant gossip. We must come together in a new way: Consciously, politically. Our stories are of individuals, but only as they are told collectively do they move us forward.

In the process of telling our stories as a conscious, political act, we begin to define ourselves and our reality. We cease, thenceforth, to be defined by the men who run our churches, by the corporations who project our images, or by the men in Washington who seek to control our destinies.

The Hebrews told their stories as a conscious political act in order to define themselves over against the dominant cultures of their day. The early Christians who preserved the stories of Jesus paid for these political acts with their lives. They told the story of Jesus in such a way as to set Him over against the imperial, emperor worshipping cult of Rome. The story was so powerful that Rome had finally to coopt it in establishing Christianity as a state religion under the emperor Constantine. Women were part of the power of that early story. Perhaps that is why it was so subversive of both established religion and the state. Women were the first to tell the world of the events of the resurrection. They traveled around as preachers and teachers of the new message, refusing to play the tradition-bound roles of breeder and domestic.

Subversive language, however, has to be constantly reinvented because it is continually being coopted by the powerful. We can no longer afford to use some of this language; for example, the royal male language for God, nor the language of the "blood of the lamb" or the "suffering servant" for Jesus. Cut off from the socio-political context which charged original Christian language with its significance, that language, in the hands of a male-dominated clergy, used by churches which reinforce powerful business interests and ally themselves with the state, has become a weapon of cultural imperialism. Notice how the emerging coalition of the Right — composed of John Birchers, the Ku Klux Klan, large insurance companies and frightened housewives — is using the language and institutions of Christianity against everything that Jesus stood for: Against the implicit faithfulness found among the pariahs of His time (in our age it is the gays); against the strength,

courage and independence of women; against the rights of the poor and oppressed; against communities of new families, formed for the purpose of sustaining one another even though they may not be related by blood.

So much of the old language has been corrupted beyond recognition that we must write our own dictionary from the words which express best our own experience and the experience of the as yet unarticulated lives of our sisters past and present. This does not mean that we throw out the Christian tradition. On the contrary, what we must do is learn to reappropriate that faith history in a new way. Some language will have to be discarded; other language turned inside out. But we cannot find the handles of reappropriation until we have gone through the process of collective, politicized storytelling and the collection of language for a new dictionary.

In the process of collective storytelling we begin to see patterns; networks of oppression connecting women in Harlan, Ky. with women in Altoona, Pa. and upstate New York. If we go far enough, we unravel the skein which leads us back to our great grandmothers, across the country to women in Chicago and on the Cheyenne Indian reservation in Wyoming, to women in the Bantustans of South Africa and women in the countrysides of Puerto Rico and Chile. We begin to ask ourselves: Why these patterns of defeat? Why after a century of struggle is our land more devastated than ever; why after the advent of birth control and women's liberation are more 13, 14, and 15-year-olds having babies than ever before and why are women in Puerto Rico, New York, on Indian reservations and in Appalachia being sterilized in large numbers? Why are women, as a group, losing ground according to every socio-economic indicator available? Recognizing that our oppression is so widespread, our defeats so redundant, relativizes our suffering. We no longer feel ashamed of our failure to live up to the individualized standards set by the men in Washington or Madison Avenue, knowing that our oppression is a small part of the systematized repression of the majority of the earth's people.

Such knowledge is powerful. We begin to identify not with the privileged, whom we have always been taught to emulate, but with the common people of the earth. It was such identification Jesus talked about in His Sermon on the Mount. A colonialist church has never been able to understand the meaning of those passages which speak of the first being last and the meek inheriting the earth. Such knowledge is the beginning of wisdom, who is personified in the Old Testament as a woman, wild and unladylike, shouting aloud in the streets for bread and justice because no one in the synagogues, the courts or the legislature would listen.

As we collect our stories they begin to shape themselves into a body of experience — a kind of litany — which can no longer be denied. They become the means for a collective self-expression which feeds and strengthens those who are able to hear, just as the stories of the Hebrews in bondage in Egypt, in flight and in temporary restitution, repeated generation after generation, have strengthened the diaspora. Just as the stories of Jesus, told and retold, sustained the early Christian community through persecution.

Through the telling and retelling of our stories, the inessentials are gradually sloughed off — those inessentials like varied colors and shapes of leaves — until only the veins, the life-bearing vessels, remain. It is then that we begin to see the patterns of triumph, steadfastness, salvation, and liberation inherent in them. As the early Hebrews and early Christians looked back over their lives and discovered these patterns, so we discover what it was in women's experience which has kept women going through tragedy and devastation, through the daily rituals of feeding and caring. We discover the secret which keeps hope more alive in the oppressed who are conscious of the source of their oppression than in those who do the oppressing. Only then can we name that which has brought us through as the God of our experience, and distinguish with any clarity the true prophets from the false.

The process of discovering and naming that God is the process of our own liberation or salvation.

As we redefine ourselves through the telling of our stories, discover the sources and patterns of our oppression, and name the God of *our* salvation, we begin to reappropriate the Christian tradition and the special folkways in which it was transmitted in a way which is truly empowering and liberating.

Perhaps when Appalachian women begin to share the stories of how their sons were dragged off to a war in South East Asia, fought to propitiate the American male god of power, they can identify with that Sarah of ancient times who watched in the same immobilized way as her husband, Abraham, took the son of her old age to the mountains as an offering, in the mistaken notion that God demands the sacrifice of the innocents for the sins of the guilty.

Perhaps when black women share stories of how their sons and husbands were taken from them through slavery, hunger, dope, war and the criminal justice system, they can gain strength through remembering Hagar, Abraham's concubine, who, through the jealousy of Sarah, was banished to the wilderness with her infant son but because of her faithfulness was promised by God that her son would live to establish a nation.

Perhaps when Appalachian women begin to share stories of their aunts who, driven from the farms to the cities during the Depression, ended up as prostitutes — the only job they could get which would pay them enough to send some back home — only then perhaps will we truly identify with the woman of ill-repute, who bathed Jesus' feet with her tears and whose implicit faithfulness has become a part of the record of salvation.

Perhaps when the day comes that black and white women, poor and middle class women are able to share their stories — and through that sharing to discover the painful contradictions of women's existence in a patriarchal, competitive and profit-oriented society — then, perhaps, there can be a reconciliation between Sarah, the wife, and Hagar, the concubine.

When we have brought to consciousness, articulated, and honed to the essentials the stories of our bondage and liberation, then we can reconnect with the buried traditions in our own folk history. No people are ever willingly, or without resistance, colonized. We should learn to look for those remnants of resistance which are often disguised as passivity, stubbornness, hostility, and superstition. We can use that wonderful democratic tradition of "testifying" in church to talk about how the coal and textile companies, the family planning experts and the welfare officials are keeping women down, and how, by participating in that sit-in at the welfare office, we are able to get food in our stomachs and spirit for our souls. We can take all those marvelous hymns which give us the shivers when we sing them and change the words around: changing the "I's" to "we's," the male pronouns to generic ones, the "blood of the Savior," to the blood of our sisters and brothers killed in the mines and the floods, and those mansions in the sky by-and-by to the green rolling hills of West Virginia. We can rediscover the forgotten heroines imbedded in our history and name them in our services when it comes time for a recollection of the saints.

◼

The Search for God In the Political Struggle

by Pablo Richard

In the 13th Century B.C., the Israelites are in Egypt as a working people. The king of Egypt is afraid of this labor force. It is so large that its members might rise up against his interests. A war would put the system of domination in crisis and the slaves would be able to take advantage of this to rebel. To hinder all possible subversion Pharaoh decides to oppress and super-exploit this slave people:

> And he said to his people, "Behold, the people of Israel are too many and too mighty for us. Come, let us deal shrewdly with them, lest they multiply, and, if war befall us, they join our enemies and fight against us and escape from the land." Therefore they set taskmasters over them to afflict them with heavy burdens; and they built for Pharaoh store cities, Pithom and Raamses. But the more they were oppressed, the more they multiplied and the more they spread abroad. And the Egyptians were in dread of the people of Israel. So they made the people of Israel serve with rigor, and made their lives bitter with hard service, in mortar and brick, and in all kinds of work in the field; in all their work they made them serve with rigor. (Exodus 1:9-14)

There is only one step between the super-exploitation of labor and genocide. The king takes that step and orders all newborn males to be killed. This order exposes the crimes carried out every day by super-exploitation (cf. Ex. 1:15-22).

HOPE EMERGES

When a people's slavery becomes intolerable the leaders appear whom the people need in order to become free:

> One day, when Moses had grown up, he went out to his people and looked on their burdens; and he saw an Egyptian beating a Hebrew, one of his people. He looked this way and that, and seeing no one he killed the Egyptian and hid him in the sand. . . . When Pharaoh heard of it, he sought to kill Moses. (Exodus 2:11-12, 15)

Moses is not a slave; by adoption he belongs to the king's family. Frequently in history the leaders of an exploited people belong to a different class. But they

Pablo Richard is a Chilean Catholic living in exile in Paris. From 1970-73 he was director of Christians for Socialism in Chile. The above was excerpted from a longer article titled "Search for God in the Political Struggle of Liberation" which first appeared in English translation in the Newspacket of N.Y. CIRCUS, April, 1978.

do not become leaders of the people until they make a radical definitive break with their own class.

Moses begins to discover the situation of slavery of his brothers and sisters but he does not commit himself to them or break off definitively with his class until he goes into action and kills an Egyptian. The act doesn't mean anything to the people; in fact, it causes a negative reaction. But for Moses personally it has great importance. No leader can demand that the people understand his personal situation, however important it may be.

> And the people of Israel groaned under their bondage, and cried out for help, and their cry under bondage came up to God. And God heard their groaning, and God remembered His covenant with Abraham, with Isaac, and with Jacob. And God saw the people of Israel, and God knew their condition. (Exodus 2:23-25)

The cry of exploited people, because of their exploitation, is something that hurts, something we never want to hear. The cries are curses, insults, blasphemies and unbearable groans. When exploitation degrades people they protest like degraded beings, not the way "decent" people would. The slave people experience the nearness of God. God hears their protest. He is not scandalized by the anger or indignation of the exploited people.

This discovery of the God-who-hears-rebellion expresses a first becoming aware, a first hope: If God hears, liberation is possible. And vice versa, if liberation is possible, it is because there is a God who hears us.

Moses, the leader, also hears the cry of the slaves and this desperate cry leads him to God. But the leader, out ahead of the people, discovers a God who not only hears but who has a strategy of liberation for the people. A higher degree of awareness leads him to a deeper experience of God:

> Then the Lord said, "I have seen the affliction of My people who are in Egypt, and have heard their cry because of their taskmasters; I know their sufferings, and I have come down to deliver them out of the hand of the Egyptians, and to bring them up out of that land to a good and broad land, a land flowing with milk and honey. . . . Come, I will send you to the Pharaoh that you may bring forth My people, the children of Israel, out of Egypt." (Exodus 3:7-8, 10)

It is impossible for rich people to hear the God of the Exodus unless they give up their riches. The mighty of this world will not discover this God who listens to the "rabble" and makes subversive plans against the established order. Only exploited people can discover the God of the Exodus. Nor is it easy to be a leader. In the struggle for liberation a person triumphs or dies. Before leading his people, Moses has to settle accounts with himself.

No leader is worthy of carrying out liberating violence unless the leader has first done liberating violence to him/herself, in his/her own heart. Within himself Moses has to subdue the coward, the deserter, the hidden accomplice of exploitation which dwells within him. The more Moses tries to master himself the better he comes to know this intransigent God whose liberating disposition cannot be detained.

The better Moses knows this intransigent God the more willing he is to struggle:

> But Moses said to the Lord, "Oh, my Lord, I am not eloquent, either heretofore or since thou has spoken to thy servant; but I am slow of speech and of tongue." Then the Lord said to him, "Who has made man's mouth? Who makes him dumb, or deaf, or seeing, or blind? Is it not I, the Lord? Now therefore go, and I will be with your mouth and teach you what you shall speak." (Exodus 4:10-12)

Moses can no longer look back. The impatience of the people shows him the impatience of God. When he manages to dominate his personal insecurity, Moses discovers the liberating design of God. The divine experience can only be, Go Forward! Having passed through the crisis of leadership Moses becomes an "agitator for subversion." He acts in an orderly, planned way, adapting to the social structure of the Hebrew people at that time. ■

A Statement of Challenge

We are 200 Christians, mostly white and university-trained, predominantly from the Northeast and Midwest states, who gathered to hear the challenge of black, feminist, and Latin American liberation theologies, and the challenge of the Native American world-view. More than hearing, however, we gathered to begin a process of response, rooted in our own experience, and directed to our own responsibilities. We want to share something of our time together with the wider Church, and to hold ourselves accountable for what we heard, said and decided.

We are part of God's people, called to respond in our own specific situations to God's command to love through our struggle for justice and nourished by God's promise that we can share in the divine endeavor to create "a new heaven and a new earth." (Rev. 21:1) We see both the command and the promise focused in the event of Jesus Christ, through whom God has entered into our experience to judge and redeem our efforts. Our hope is founded on the power He incarnates — a hope that does not diminish our responsibility but heightens it, since it frees us from trusting solely in our own power and enables us to act in the confidence that "with God all things are possible," beyond whatever we ask or think or achieve . . .

Excerpted from the document issued by a workshop sponsored by the Alternative Theology Project of Theology in the Americas, June 17-19, 1978.

I. THE CHALLENGE

. . .Black theology challenged us to take the religion of poor people seriously, and to question the theological criteria that validate only certain people and certain language as theological. It challenged us also to understand that love is the controlling element of power, not its opposite or its exclusion; and to deepen our understanding of how racism is interwoven with, and supported by, classism, colonialism and sexism.

The challenge came from Latin American to reject the claim that there are "owners of theology"; to hear challenges to our traditional theology made from a libertarian perspective; to affirm the right of oppressed people to do their own theology and to reappropriate the Bible from their viewpoint; to stress the priority of the "rights of the poor" and not simply abstract "human rights"; to affirm a theology of life whose vision of resurrection first passes through the real and concrete death of countless poor people in the Third World.

We were challenged to listen to the voice of "those who hold up half the sky," the women of the world; to probe the social roots of modern feminism and the systematic destruction of women's culture in the modern period, rooted in the process of industrialization and in a false philosophical dualism of mind and body; to be bold in the face of a powerful socio-cultural backlash against the emergence of women, a backlash that signals a new stage of capitalism and is nourished in some powerful sectors of the churches.

And finally we heard the liberating challenge of the Native American world-view to examine the basic assumptions of industrialization and of social movements; to ponder the Indians' rootedness in, and respect for, land as one's immediate environment in the face of the plunder of the earth's resources; to affirm community and relationships over against individualism; and to probe the unity of identity and environment, and the personal nature of all the universe.

Having heard these challenges, we turned to the search for ways to understand and respond. Our response took the form of both structural analysis and theological reflection; a structural analysis of the new stage global capitalism is now entering, and how it will affect us and our people; a theological reflection on what this means for our own lives as Christians, especially in the light of our bondage, the false values that constitute the myth of the "middle class," and our allegiance to religious symbols we often use uncritically.

II. STRUCTURAL ANALYSIS

Reflecting on our experience in the '60s has forced us to a new assessment, and an exploration of new directions for creating love through justice, since the decade that promised so much did not produce the anticipated fruits. We believe there were significant achievements: A new sensitivity to the depths of the struggle against racism and sexism emerged, and a war, however tardily, was stopped. But we underestimate the brutality and global nature of the forces ranged against resistance to injustice. Our theological commitments were related to a faulty political analysis not grounded in economics. Could a more penetrating political-economic analysis help us to act more adequately for justice in the future? . .

. . .We are entering a new period in the life of global capitalism, and this new period will bring hard times upon our people, a profound ecological crisis, and frightening challenges for the churches. We are entering a new period of industrialization, characterized by highly mobile transnational capital and a technology that increasingly uses machines and computers (capital-intensive) and requires less and less people. All this results in a new world system in which working people of every city, state, region and country are forced to bid against each other in the sale of their labor power; a new world system in which large margins of populations are no longer needed, resulting in high and abiding unemployment, a reserve labor pool to weaken workers' bargaining power; a new world system in which inflation will not go away, but steadily undercuts the social gains of ordinary people; a new world system of increasing repression to stifle dissent and deny basic human needs.

The new attack on working people comes economically in the attempt to cut real wages and reduce social services. The political attack is seen as the rise of a new Right Wing and its alliance with major big business sectors, which are launching a structural attack on women, minorities, labor and the poor — a situation too frequently legitimated by church structures and leaders. Culturally, we see the attack in the rising blame put on the victims of the crisis — the poor, minorities, and women — and in the promotion of a new ethic of discipline and austerity that abandons ordinary people and their basic needs.

All this, for the so-called "middle class," means the beginning of permanent and confusing downward mobility from relative comfort and security to awkward economic adjustments and new insecurities. It is time for discovering that while upward mobility and affluence have been realized by a few, they are now a cruel deceit for the sectors of the labor force, especially hourly-rated workers. The new situation means harsher working conditions, decline of safety standards, and deepening exploitation. But most important, for the poor it means inadequate

education, no jobs, rising malnutrition and rates of infant mortality, sickness and death. The harsh burden of the new stage falls especially on the young and the old, on women, and on minorities.

In defense against this attack, and in the struggle for a new society, we discover that ordinary working people are finding new forms of solidarity — coalitions of labor, the poor, women, minorities, sensitive professionals and church groups.

For religious eyes, this new structural stage of capitalism which absolutizes the maximization of profits, appears as an idol, a violation of the First Commandment, for it demands human sacrifice to preserve the system.

For some of us, such an analysis is new. Many have not been used to looking at the world structurally. But we feel drawn to pursue the analysis and to explore what new directions our lives and our work in institutions must take in response. Others among us are familiar with this analysis and seek to deepen our grasp of it. All of us sense that capitalism is the fundamental problem. While we can speak of three interpretations of our present crisis, a conservative, a liberal, and a radical, we are seeking to probe the radical analysis. We suspect that conservative and liberal analyses are being found wanting — they do not serve the majority's basic needs, and chiefly benefit the dominant classes. For some, this means a search for as yet undiscovered alternative social structures that will be more just. For others it means a struggle for a humanistic socialism. We intend to test our analysis and our imagination, believing that alternative social structures can be constructed that will be more responsive to basic human needs than are our present ones. While we have no immediate program and no easy answers, we feel drawn to test these paths.

We know that such testing will have its price, that it asks for painful and unknown changes within ourselves, our families, our churches and our interpretations of the gospel, as well as within the social structures of which we are presently a part.

III. THEOLOGICAL REFLECTION

A full confrontation with these realities forces us not only to look for new political strategies but also to engage in a deeper confrontation with our faith. We realize that our reading of Scripture and our tradition has been distorted by class-based, racist, sexist and nationalist perspectives. We are forced into a re-reading, by our sisters and brothers from other parts of the human family, and we are discovering fresh ways to see God acting in the world, ways previously hidden from us.

We are learning that the God of the Bible has unambiguously taken sides with the poor, and calls the high and mighty to account. This is the same God who became incarnate in one of "the poor of the land," Jesus of Nazareth, who in the midst of announcing the Kingdom of God, made the cause of the poor His own and died in solidarity with them victimized by the powerful, to whom He was a radical threat.

When we read of the Exodus from Egypt, we cannot escape the conviction that we may be numbered among those who serve in Pharaoh's court. Then we confront the Biblical insistence that to know God is to do justice (Jeremiah 22:13-16), we realize that we may be convicted thereby of disbelief; for if we are not doing justice, we do not know God. When we are confronted by the claim that the true fast, the true worship, is to feed the hungry and break the yoke of oppression (Isaiah 58), we realize that many of us fail to honor God in the way God asks. Conversely, when we confront so-called "secular analyses" of the systematic nature of evil in our society, which pit the oppressor class against the oppressed, we discover that these analyses have an undergirding in the prophets and the message of Jesus Himself.

What is "good news to the poor" (Luke 4:8, cf. Isaiah 61) may seem initially to be bad news to the non-poor, yet we must hear that devastating word before we can truly hear the gospel's liberating word to us, which is that we need not remain bound and captivated by consumer-oriented values, myths of upward mobility, fear of living in a nation that is no longer "number one." Our trust need no longer be in those things, but in the God who brings down the mighty from their thrones and exalts those of low degree (Luke 1:46-55).

We feel called to challenge the way our religious symbols have been distorted, both by us and by our culture, to give religious sanction to capitalist society — a way of life that benefits the few at increasing cost to the many, that legitimates the pursuit of profit above concern for persons, and that co-opts a God of justice into the sanctifier of an unjust *status quo*. We must root out such profanities, especially when they have been legitimated by the religious communities of which we are a part.

In this effort, our engagement and struggle with the working poor people of our own country will help us define a new path for our faith. This indicates a need to restore the central Christian concepts and symbols — truth, power, community, love, the Eucharist, cross and resurrection, the Spirit — to the service of people in their concrete struggles for a fundamentally different future. We must relocate these symbols within the horizon of Biblical understanding and link our celebration of faith to on-going daily struggles for survival, resistance and change. In such efforts to end false worship, which promotes injustice and invites submission to the idolatry of capitalism, we seek to be faithful in creative obedience to the God of history.

This means that while our agenda can be easily described, it is awesomely difficult to enact: *It means shifting from alleviation of the results of poverty to elimination of the causes of poverty.* It means challenging our society's easy acquiescence in a system that leaves one-third of the human family well fed, one-third hungry and one-third doomed to die prematurely. It means challenging the complicity of our churches in this acquiescence. Rather than reflecting the present world our churches are called upon to become the *transformed* world, in which the imperative for radical change can be embodied in the name of the God who brought Israel out of bondage (Exodus 20), the God whose righteousness is exhibited in an overriding concern for justice . . .

. . . Such reflections demand the creation of new personal and community life-styles, and "next steps" that we must take as we leave the conference. We all need to be in closer contact and solidarity with the labor movement, and with individual workers, from whom our positions of relative privilege have isolated us. We need to find others, both individuals and groups, with whom to link our efforts so that a network of those committed to a radical restructuring of our society may be developed. We seek to

do as much of this as possible within our existing church structures, but by no means to limit ourselves to those. We need to continue challenging theologies that legitimate human exploitation, and searching for a theology and commitment to a socialist alternative that can be honestly explored and critically embraced.

∎

A Message to the Black Church & Community

THE MESSAGE OF BLACK THEOLOGY

We speak from the perspective we call Black Theology: *Black* — because our enslaved foreparents appropriated the Christian Gospel and articulated its relevance to our freedom struggle with incisive accents that black women and men have sounded ever since. *Theology* — because our people's perception of human life and history begins with God, who works in the person of Jesus Christ for liberation from every bondage.

Therefore, Black Theology is "Godtalk" that reflects the black Christian experience of God's

action and our grateful response. Black Theology understands the "good news" as freedom and Jesus Christ as the Liberator.

Black Theology is formulated from our reading the Bible as we experience our suffering as a people. Black Theology moves between our churches and our community: The Church proclaims the message and the message reverberates back upon the Church, enhanced by the religious consciousness of black people, including those who stand outside of the institutional Church but are not beyond God's grace and His revelation.

The God of Moses and Joshua, of sister Ruth and brother Amos, of our African ancestors and our slave forebearers, has revealed Himself in Jesus Christ, the Black Messiah. He has heard the cry of our people, captive to the racist structures of this

Excerpted from a document drafted and adopted by the national conference of the Black Theology Project of Theology in the Americas, Atlanta, Georgia, August 1977.

land, and is come to deliver us as He came to Israel of old in Egypt-land. In our day, the blackness of Jesus is a religious symbol of oppression and deliverance from oppression; of His struggle and victory over principalities, powers and wickedness in the high places of this age.

FAILURE OF TRADITIONAL CHRISTIANITY

We cannot affirm the present religious situation in the USA. One of the greatest tragedies of American Christianity has been its failure to comprehend the physical as well as spiritual nature of human beings. With few exceptions, the Church has attempted to address the spiritual needs of people while negating their physical and material requirements. Traditional theology has failed to see that ultimate salvation and historical liberation are inseparable aspects of the indivisible gospel of Jesus.

We disassociate ourselves from such piecemeal Christianity. Any gospel that speaks the Truth of God in the black community must deal with the issues of life here and now as well as with the transcendent dimension of the proclamation. The gospel cannot surrender to blind tradition or emotional effusion that render people insensible to the pain and conflict of earthly experience.

The Church must come out from behind its stained-glass walls and dwell where mothers are crying, children are hungry, and fathers are jobless. The issue is survival in a society that has defined blackness as corruption and degradation. Jesus did not die in a sanctuary, nor did Martin Luther King, Jr. In those places where pain was the deepest and suffering the most severe, there Jesus lived and suffered, died and was resurrected.

As long as innocent children continue to die in tenement fires, as long as families have to live in winter without heat, hot water and food, as long as people are forced to live with rats and roaches, the gospel must be heard in judgment against the disorder of society, and the Church has a responsibility — not to point people to the future life when all troubles will cease, but to help them overcome their powerlessness, rise up and take charge of their lives.

POWER OF THE BLACK CHURCH

We reject the notion that the black church has no power. Each and every week, black ministers interact with more people than do any other community leaders. Indeed, many black ministers have limited their roles to visiting the sick, burying the dead, marrying the lovers and presiding over institutional trivia, while leaving responsibility for real social change to politicians and social agencies whom they feel to be more qualified than themselves. But the black preacher is still the natural leader and the black church continues to be the richest source of ethically motivated leadership, lay and clergy, in our community.

The black church must re-assert its power to transform our neighborhoods into communities. Our church possesses gospel power which must be translated into community power, for there can be no authentic community in a condition of powerlessness.

We are concerned also about people whose desperation is not abject material poverty but poverty of soul and spirit. We do not believe that better jobs and bigger houses, color televisions and latest model cars prove that people have attained the abundant life of which Jesus spoke. That abundant life cannot be experienced by a people captive to the idolatry of a sensate and materialistic culture.

We abhor the capitulation of some of our people to values based on the assumptions that things make for security and that distance from the distressed masses makes for a trustworthy barricade against the racism that holds us all in contempt. Commitment to physical gratification as the purpose of life and voidance of the gospel's moral, ethical standards provide false foundations for hard choices. Such false values divide and separate a people who would be free.

The identification of black liberation with the material success of a few, physically and mentally severed from the black masses, makes mockery of the unity essential for the salvation of us all. Even the material good fortune of that few is poisoned by emptiness and isolation from the people's struggle without which the mission of Jesus Crhist can be neither understood nor undertaken.

ROOTS OF THE CRISIS

The issue for all of us is survival. The root problem is human *sinfulness* which nurtures monopolistic capitalism, aided by racism and abetted by sexism.

Our crisis is spiritual, material and moral. Black people seem unable to effectively counter disruptive forces that undermine our quality of life. We seem unable to collectively define our situation, rediscover the nature of our problems, and develop sustained coalitions that can resolve our dilemmas.

Exploitative, profit-oriented capitalism is a way of ordering life fundamentally alien to human value in general and to black humanity in particular. Racism and capitalism have set the stage for despoilation of natural and human resources all around the world. Yet those who seriously challenge these systems are often effectively silenced. We view racism as criminality and yet we are called the criminals. We view racism as a human aberration, yet we are called the freaks. The roots of our crisis are in social, economic, media and political power systems that prevent us from managing the reality of our everyday lives.

It is this intolerable, alien order that has driven us to Atlanta seeking a word from the Lord out of the wellsprings of black theological tradition.

The black church tradition of service to its people is documented in our history books, our poetry, our drama and our worship. This tradition will not permit us to separate ourselves from our African heritage which is characterized by the sharing of resources and talents by all. Therefore, the black church and the community which it serves are one in the Spirit of God, who does not differentiate between the secular and the sacred and who binds us inseparably to one another.

Our victimization by the rich, the powerful, and the greedy makes it necessary for us to continually renew the tradition of our forebearers who stood in the foreground of the struggle for freedom. *The black church is the only institution over which black people have total control.* That church must remain in service among black people wherever they may reside.

That Church must be one with and inseparable

from our brothers and sisters around the world who fight for liberation in a variety of ways, including armed struggle. We affirm whatever methods they decide best in their particular situations and make no pious and hypocritical judgments which condemn those efforts to bring an end to their oppression, recognizing that we in this country have ourselves been compelled to make similar choices and may be so compelled again.

Because of racism and imperialism, domestic and foreign, we black people are an international community of outlaws and aliens in our respective homelands and in those communities where we have chosen or been forced to reside. The living servanthood of the black church has been and is, today, an inescapable necessity. Therefore, we do not reject the disinherited, for they are us. We do not reject the disenfranchised, for they are us.

Rather we embrace all of God's children who hunger and thirst for justice and human dignity. We rededicate and recommit ourselves, and the black churches in whose leadership we participate, to the struggle for freedom from injustice, racism and oppression. This we declare to be the essential meaning of Black Theology as defined by those who conceive it, nurture it and affirm it as a source of inspiration and reflective action for all black people and for all the exploited and oppressed peoples of the world who are grasped by its truth for their situations.

HOPE OF THE FUTURE

Here in Atlanta, as we have struggled over ideas and realities, as we have worshiped in the black tradition, we have felt ourselves surrounded by a great cloud of witnesses. Richard Allen, David Walker, Nat Turner, Henry MacNeil Turner, Sojourner Truth, Harriet Tubman, Henry H. Garnet, Frederick Douglas, W.E.B. DuBois, Marcus Garvey, Malcolm X, Martin Luther King, Ralph Featherstone, Paul Robeson, Fannie Lou Hamer — the innumerable hosts of our ancestors, heroes unknown and unsung. Their blood cries out from the ground. They endured trials and tribulation; braved hate-crazed mobs; were attacked, beaten and lynched; watched loved ones killed before their eyes without surrendering their integrity or dignity as they took up the cross of struggle. Of them this world is not worthy.

In their company and in the company of generations yet unborn, whose life and liberty will be shaped by our deeds, we call upon our Church and our community to join us in the warfare that shall know no end, until we shall be perfected together in that kingdom of justice, love and peace which moves relentlessly towards us by the dominion of Jesus the Christ, our Lord and Liberator. ∎

A Message to the Hispanic Community

We are a group of 60 Hispanic Christian men and women. Among the Protestants, we represent eight denominations. As a whole, we include ordained men and women and lay persons, community organizers, teachers, church bureaucrats, social scientists and farmworkers. We are also Mexican-Americans, Chicanos, Mexicans, Puerto Ricans, Cubans, as well as immigrants from Spain and other Latin American and Caribbean countries. Universal race that we are, we run the gamut of skin colors, since we are blacks, whites, mulattoes and *mestizos.* What a beautiful people we are!

OUR REALITY

We do not want to appear hopeless romantics. The obstacles that might have prevented this communion for us are still real. Not long ago, as Protestants and Catholics we denied each other's Christian identity. Such antagonisms have left their mark on our catechisms and in much other literature still in circulation. Even worse, that mark is still to be found in painful memories, in injured spirits, in alienated communities and in divided families (I Corinthians 11:18).

On the other hand, our very history as diverse Hispanic groups is still a source of disagreement. It is unreasonable to hope that Chicanos and Puerto Ricans, humiliated for centuries by dominant groups in this country, should display the kind of gratitude and national solidarity that recent Cuban immigrants have shown as a result of being welcomed and given help. Nor is it reasonable to suppose that those who have already "made it" within the "American dream" should display the same anger as those of our people who have been battered against the walls of prejudice. Similar conflicts exist between our unrepentant "machos" and our new feminists, between the academic intellectuals and those who struggle at the most basic level of human existence, between those who have been tamed by the churches and those who have been liberated by their faith, between those who are comfortable and those who are poor, between those who are articulate and those who are tongue-

tied, between those highly schooled from south of the Rio Bravo and those still unschooled from north of the border or vice-versa.

It is natural for these very real differences to heighten when we are confronted with the challenge of taking stands *vis-a-vis* the disastrous condition of the vast majority of our Hispanic people. We deliberately designed this Hispanic theological and ecumenical consultation around the realities of oppression and liberation among our people (Ex. 20:2). The following were presented with documentation as illustrative case-studies:

1. The struggle of C.O.P.S. (Communities Organized for Public Service) to force the municipal and private authorities of San Antonio to honor their institutional obligations toward all citizens, especially in the poor neighborhoods that are overwhelmingly made up of Chicanos.
2. The battle of F.L.O.C. (Farm Labor Organizing Committee in the Midwest), a Chicano farmworkers' organization, which continues its struggle not so much against the ranch owners but against the multi-national corporations that buy up and control their harvests.
3. The organizing work and the use of economic, social, educational and housing pressure exerted by the Latin American Coalition of Lakeview, in Chicago.
4. The efforts toward full liberation by P.R.I.S.A. of Puerto Rico, an ecumenical group that is trying, along with other national and international groups, to offer alternatives to the disastrous North American colonialism that began in Puerto Rico with the military invasion of 1898.
5. The courageous activities of the refugee groups called Christian Cubans for Justice and Freedom, which advocates the normalization of diplomatic relations between the United States and Cuba along with the lifting of the blockade, while simultaneously raising the problem of political prisoners in Cuba and framing its action within a democratic socialist context.
6. The firmness of the Texas Farmworker Union, which with meager resources is struggling for the rights of agricultural workers against the overwhelming power of landowners and the collusion of state and Federal authorities.

In all these cases the abuse of power by those who run the institutions and the economy is clear. Even clearer are the brutalizing contradictions of a capitalist system in crisis that requires unemployment, cheap labor, equally cheap raw materials, the transformation of luxuries into "necessities," the disappearance of free enterprise, the accumulation of vast wealth by a smaller and smaller minority, consumption as the primary goal in life, and the sacrifice of human beings on the altar of profits.

Perhaps for the first time, in spite of our political and ideological differences, most of us at the confer-

From a document issued by the Hispanic Ecumenical Theological Project of Theology in the Americas following a conference in San Antonio, October 24-28, 1978.

ence did not hesitate to point to this capitalism in crisis as the principal cause, or at least an important cause, not only of persistent economic poverty, so disproportionate among our people, but also of the spiritual poverty of those who have increased their economic advantage at peril to their souls. It was not surprising that this realization could lead some of us to think of what would have been unthinkable in the past: Either a radical transformation of this economic system, or its replacement by another system. It should be understood that this, being new ground for us, is in some ways unsettling, for we may appear naive or subversive. But since the focus of our theological reflection was the rich Christ who becomes poor (Philippians 2:5-9), and the poor as the chief embodiment of Christ (Matthew 25:31-46), how is it possible to evade the economic question?

We sincerely believe we cannot evade it. Otherwise, our understanding of the Hispanic reality in this country would be very limited. We could not be taken seriously when we say that we are in solidarity with the undocumented immigrants, with the farmers of Ohio, Texas and California, with the indigent of the South Bronx of New York, the West Side of San Antonio, the East Side of Los Angeles, or Lakeview in Chicago, or with the defenseless inhabitants of Vieques in Puerto Rico under the occupation of the United States Navy, or the suffering Nicaraguans who have been attacked to the point of genocide by the Somozan dictatorship that has been supported by the American government.

We do not wish to blame others and avoid confronting our own responsibility. We think it is imperative to engage in self-criticism as well; it is part of our confession of faith as sinners (I John 1:8-9). Cultural shock and the mirage of a consumer society lead some of us to aggressiveness, escapism and social maladaptation. We acknowledge a lack of unity among Hispanic groups, a provincialism of vision, a personality cult among our leaders, and a slowness on our part to contribute to the social and political struggle. We also acknowledge that "machismo" is still a reality in the Hispanic communities and that we have not formed coalitions with other minority groups, especially with the black and Native American communities in this country.

We are not assuming that we have reached definitive conclusions concerning political and economic systems that would be more compatible with obedience to the Christ of the poor, or the defense of Christ's poor. What we do affirm is that if Christian love is to be effective (James 1:15-17) we must unite with others who are struggling to make political and economic democracy a reality, no matter what terminology is used. What we do know is that we have some political democracy and less and less economic democracy.

RE-READING THE BIBLE

The miracle of faith we experienced ecumenically at San Antonio in spite of our pluralism and the complexity of ideological differences, came about from our re-reading the Bible as the revelation of God written chiefly from the experience of suffering and oppression and offered to us for our own full liberation. What happiness we felt in the course of our reflection, that the book that had separated us in the past was uniting us in the present, Catholics and Protestants alike! We also believe that we have come to a better understanding of what the Latin American theologians of liberation mean when they tell us that with respect to the Bible, the poor are in a position of "hermeneutical privilege," which is to say, they are in a privileged situation to know God. This is a way of affirming that the lowest have immediate access to the Biblical God who from lowliness liberates Israel from captivity (Exodus 22:21-24), who raises up prophets as defenders of the poor (Jeremiah 1:4-10), who becomes incarnate as Galilean in Jesus Christ, who eats and drinks with "nobodies," who is crucified because He is a threat to the oppressors, and who guarantees by His resurrection that there will be a day without tears, in which death will be no more, a day without crying or pain (Revelation 21:1-4).

The re-reading of the Bible has led us toward a new understanding of Jesus as Lord and Savior (Colossians 1:15-20). By confessing our faith in Him, from our vantage point as Hispanics in the United States, we began a re-formulation of our theology in contrast to the dominant theology we have received.

In our time together we have reflected on two aspects of our Christology:

First, we have re-affirmed our faith in the saving action of God through Jesus Christ and its continuation in the midst of the ecclesial community. Western thought has turned Christocentrism into Christo-exclusivism.

Our communitarian culture and tradition are impelling us to discover the social dimension of our faith and the role of Jesus and ourselves in a community of faith, praise and commitment.

Second, we have re-read the saving action of Jesus from the perspective of our condition as poor and oppressed people in a rich country like the United States.

Jesus and the apostles were Galileans, spurned by the powerful of their time. From the position of a marginal, Jesus initiates His saving work for all. He invites all to conversion and to enter into the Kingdom of His Father. But He announces that He has "to go to Jerusalem" (Luke 9:51). "To go up to Jerusalem" means to defy the center of structural power, the root of the oppression of His people. Jesus confronts the established powers with His prophetic truth and denounces with signs and with His word the abuse and corruption of the structures and the sin embodied in the social order.

Confronted with the evidence, the authorities of His time are left defenseless. Their only way out is to eliminate the prophet (John 11:50). Jesus takes up the cross. The world rejects Him. But God rejects and overpowers those who condemn Him by "raising Him up from the dead" (Acts 2:24).

From the perspective of Hispanics seeking to follow Jesus, we discover our identity and our evangelizing mission. Rejected and scorned by the powers of this country, we, like the Galileans, are chosen by God to live out and to proclaim the good news of liberation for all. Like Jesus, we must "go up to Jerusalem," to the centers of economic, political and religious power in order to denounce oppression with the strength of the truth of the gospel.

We know that the road is long and that we cannot be "greater than the Master" (John 13:16). But our faith gives us the certainty that He who raised up Jesus will raise us up also (I Thessalonians 4:14).

CHURCH AS COMMUNITY

This kind of re-reading of the Bible, based on the poor as the chief fact of faith, inevitably leads — as we discovered during this conference — to a new form of ecclesial community. Fortunately, there are already foretastes of this Church in a growing number of Hispanic congregations. We are referring to a fully liberating and prophetic Church which puts the people of God on the march. Its commitment takes into account everything that affects us as human beings. It personalizes us, so to speak, and gives us identity as special children of God who fear neither the mighty nor the demons.

It is a communitarian Church, permeated by the love of Jesus, ecumenically alive and able to live with tension and to open itself to consultation, to decisions and action in common, and to self-criticism. It has historical embodiment, taking responsibility for its past, redeeming the present, enriching itself with a cultural pluralism and engaging in immediate reforms that will lead to the future transformation both of itself and the world that surrounds it. It is a Church that listens before it proclaims and does not denounce without also announcing. Its evangelization is total, making the gospel good news in everything that has human worth. Because of this it dares to call itself the "universal sacrament of salvation," of all and for all (Revelation 21:1-4).

This Church we already foresee is one that in evangelizing is evangelized, in reforming is reformed, in being an agent of change is changed. Its horizon is the future of God, by which we mean the Kingdom of God, a present reality that is a foretaste of divine and human justice. With our eyes fixed on that horizon we do not absolutize any system, we denounce those who are opposed to the Kingdom and we critically support all who align themselves with its purposes (Revelation 3:12-13).

This is the Church we want to build (Hebrews 9:11-12): A Church that demands justice politically, equality racially, efficacious love religiously, international vision nationally, and mutuality in the relationship between men and women. Its point of departure is the poor who cling to Jahweh as their defender, and if it is first of all the defender of the poor, it is also enabled to be the defender of all. Its ministries are multiple and shared, and they involve not only ordained men and women but also those who justly organize the community, work in unions or engage in political action (I Corinthians 12:4-11). It is a pilgrim Church always seeking the city with solid foundations whose architect and builder is God (Hebrews 11:10).

We are fully aware that this Church is only in its initial stages, but it has features that are already clear enough to challenge us to continue giving it greater visibility. In any case, it already had sufficient reality to make us feel more than ever thankful to follow it as "mother and teacher." ∎

Group Exercise

Practically every paragraph of the above selections is alive with new discoveries of connections between the handed-down story of faith and the struggle of the present moment.

"The Message to the Hispanic Community" concludes with an invitation for all readers of the message to join the writers "in this pilgrimage of the people of God in solidarity with the poor." In the exercise for this session, let us seek to understand what it means for us to respond to this invitation and to give some careful examination to our social location and class commitment. Let us join in fashioning new connections between our present reality and the Christian story.

Divide your group into smaller groups of five or six participants each. In each small group mount several sheets of newsprint so that everyone can see them. Designate a reporter for each group to make note of responses for later sharing.

Spend an hour or more to consider the following questions, listing the various answers. Do not spend time disputing the accuracy of someone else's response. List all responses, even contradictory ones. The contradictions can be a fertile starting point for further discussion. Paragraph numbers noted in parentheses refer to the text of the "Hispanic message," where you can find some examples of how people in that consultation framed their responses.

1 What are some objective differences in work experience, class, sex, race, national origin, age, family life, *etc.* among those in your group which can be sources of different perspectives and attitudes regarding our economic system?

2 Given a Christian commitment to solidarity with the poor and oppressed, how are the continuing realities of oppression and liberation experienced by those within your group? (paragraphs 2, 3) List concrete examples of specific struggles against oppression in which you are involved. (paragraph 4)

3 What is the role of our economic system and class structure in the oppression you experience? (paragraphs 5, 6)

4 In what ways do you share responsibility for the continuing oppression of yourself and others? (paragraph 8)

5 How does the saving/liberating work of Jesus speak to your situation? What does it mean for you "to go to Jerusalem") (paragraphs 10-14)

6 How have you experienced "the God-who-hears-rebellion" to which Pablo Richard refers?

7 What signs do you see of the emergence of "a fully liberating and prophetic Church which puts the people of God on the march"? (paragraphs 16-18)

8 In such a prophetic Church, how can our Christian faith and tradition be reclaimed as a foundation of our united struggle for liberation? List specific examples drawn from Scripture, theology, worship, devotional practices, parish life, *etc*.

9 What "subversive language" is effective for the churches today? (See Sheila Collins' article.)

Gather all groups together and spend another hour summarizing the work of each smaller group and sharing common insights. At the end of your discussion you may want to read aloud together paragraphs 17-19 of the Hispanic Message as a collective statement of faith and hope.

A Reform Is a Reform — Or Is It?

Throughout this volume we have been reflecting on the convergence of three themes. One is the reality of personal experience. Alienation, exploitation and social injustice lead us to social consciousness. We are not alone in suffering the consequences of capitalism. Inflation, unemployment and the cutback of social services affect us all. The second is our quest for understanding. We share the need for a theoretical framework to guide our activity and to develop an analysis of the social forces that shape our lives. The third is the reclaiming of our Christian tradition. Our religious commitment to the ethical demands of the gospel requires us to struggle for justice.

The convergence of personal experience, social analysis and religious tradition marks the occasion for our involvement as makers, not just victims of history; as subjects, not just objects of human destiny; as change-agents, and not just observers and complainers.

Many of us are already involved in substantive efforts to effect constructive change within our communities. But the experience of many such efforts often carries a high cost. Seeing our actions prove ineffective, we are frustrated; our energy and enthusiasm are taxed. By underestimating the size of problems, by looking for quick victories and mostly by not bringing an adequate analysis to the task, we often become weary and discouraged. In our struggle to overcome, we have no clear standards or measure of success.

In this session we try to confront that problem. When is a reform not a reform? Why are our struggles for social justice not sufficiently productive, or sometimes even counter-productive?

We begin with a brief story about a hypothetical community and its response to the dramatic need for a rescue operation. As with many of the gospel parables, exaggeration in the story is for the purpose of emphasis. But this parable does focus on one of the more difficult choices we face — should we only minister to the victims of injustice, or also seek to cure the cause of injustice?

This story is followed by excerpts from an article by Peter Dreier, from which we take the title to this session, "A Reform Is a Reform, Or Is It?" It speaks to our predicament and suggests a solution. Following Dreier's article,

we pose five criteria with which to begin an assessment of our social practice. We tell, then, the story of a steel plant closing in Youngstown, Ohio, the unemployment crisis it caused there and the action taken by a religious coalition formed to meet this challenge. Finally, John Collins examines the struggle to reopen the plant, testing the ecumenical coalition's initiative against the proposed criteria.

To bring this discussion home, we suggest you engage in a critical evaluation of some of the struggles of people in your own group.

A PARABLE OF GOOD WORKS

Once upon a time there was a small village on the edge of a river. The people there were good and the life in the village was good. One day a villager noticed a baby floating down the river. The villager quickly jumped into the river and swam out to save the baby from drowning.

The next day this same villager was walking along the river bank and noticed two babies in the river. He called for help, and both babies were rescued from the swift waters. And the following day four babies were seen caught in the turbulent current. And then eight, then more, and still more.

The villagers organized themselves quickly, setting up watch towers and training teams of swimmers who could resist the swift waters and rescue babies. Rescue squads were soon working 24 hours a day. And each day the number of helpless babies floating down the river increased.

The villagers organized themselves efficiently. The rescue squads were now snatching many children each day. Groups were trained to give mouth-to-mouth resuscitation. Others prepared formula and provided clothing for the chilled babies. Many, particularly elderly women, were involved in making clothing and knitting blankets. Still others provided foster homes and placement.

While not all the babies, now very numerous, could be saved, the villagers felt they were doing well to save as many as they could each day. Indeed, the village priest blessed them in their good work. And life in the village continued on that basis.

One day, however, someone raised the question, "But where are all these babies coming from? Who is throwing them into the river? Why? Let's organize a team to go upstream and see who's doing it." The seeming logic of the elders countered: "And if we go upstream who will operate the rescue operations? We need every concerned person here."

"But don't you see," cried the one lone voice, "if we find out who is throwing them in, we can stop the problem and no babies will drown. By going upstream we can eliminate the cause of the problem."

"It is too risky."

And so the numbers of babies in the river increase daily. Those saved increase, but those who drown increase even more.

*   *   *

If this story were told in the style of the gospel parables, it might end with the question: "Which of these, the good-intentioned program the villagers pursued, or the rejected suggestion to go upstream, showed more concern for the children?" Certainly the gospel imperative requires us to relieve suffering — the cup of water to the thirsty, food to the hungry, and — the rescue of the drowning! But it is also evident that genuine commitment requires determining the causes of social ills and eliminating them. Good health, for society as well as for the individual, requires a diagnosis of the sources of infection, not just the treating of symptoms. Our efforts in social mission must be self-critical. It is not enough to "do good" if we can do better.

The purpose of this session is to lead us into a healthy criticism of our present commitment to "good works," to see if we can discern ways in which our efforts can be more productive and more geared toward eliminating root causes. ∎

A Reform Is a Reform, Or Is It?

by Peter Dreier

It is crucial that we have an understanding of reforms. For after all, any progressive social change short of the seizure of state power has been and will be defined as a reform. . . . The question becomes one of assessing strategies and tactics which successfully bring about important, or "structural" reforms. . . . It is necessary to assess political impact of reforms. . . . As Andre Gorz [French journalist] writes, "All struggle for reform is not necessarily reformist." Gorz defines a "reformist" reform as one within the limits of the system. On the other hand, "non-reformist," or "structural" reforms are conceived "in view of what should be made possible in terms of human needs and demands. . . . A non-reformist reform," Gorz writes, "is determined not in terms of what can be, but what should be. . . ."

Four short examples will serve to illustrate:

Passage of the Wagner Act in 1935 was the result of the fear within the ruling class of the possibility of mass radicalization. . . . And although it can be seen as a form of co-optation by the moderate wing of the ruling class, it also had the effect of making the entire movement for industrial unionism, the CIO, possible. It is an open question what long-term effect this might have had if World War II had not "resolved" the contradictions of the Depression.

The recent passage of the Occupational Safety and Health Act (OSHA) is, of course, good in itself for improving working conditions. In addition, it provides a vehicle for demanding more *worker control* over conditions. In the recent struggles of the United Mine Workers Union, conflict was not primarily over the issues of wages and pensions (which the mine owners could afford, and pass on to consumers), but over issues of health (Black Lung), mine safety, and the right to strike over safety and health issues. On these issues, mineowners were understandably reluctant to concede to union demands for worker control, which undermine the owners' authority, may result in lower productivity and may change the relations of power between the capitalist and working classes. Thus OSHA is a "transitional" reform which can raise the ability of the working class, in Lenin's words, "to fight and conquer."

On a local level, one can apply these standards to struggles of tenant unions and community groups over housing and neighborhood conditions. Many a rent strike, for example, has resulted in short term reductions of rent increases or repair of a building. Although usually this leaves the relationship between tenants and landlords the same, in some cases tenants have been able to force a landlord — often through the intervention of the local government (housing court) — to re-negotiate the lease. Tenants in these cases force the landlord to give up some of the one-sided, discretionary power which the typical lease assumes, thus changing the relations of power (though not property relations) between tenants and landlord. This is not only good in itself, but also can become the basis for coalitions among neighborhood tenants unions, and even can provide a questioning of the private property profit system itself.

In Chicago, the Citizens Action Program, a city-wide coalition of working-class neighborhood organizations, responded to the "redlining" tactics of local savings-and-loans (by which certain neighborhoods are systematically denied home improvement mortgages, thus making "neighborhood deterioration" a self-fulfilling prophecy). CAP first disclosed the "redlining" tactic to the press, picketed the savings-and-loans which were involved, and then threatened to systematically withdraw citizens' savings accounts unless the bank agreed to provide a specified amount of money for neighborhood improvement (rather than loan the local money out in the more profitable suburbs). Especially in the present liquidity crisis, local savings-and-loans could not afford this drain on their resources. The contract between community groups and savings-and-loans which results, like the tenant union-landlord and union-management agreements, changed the structural relations of power in the neighborhood. These are more than mere concessions from the power elite.

We see in these examples of reforms more than structural changes of power, but in addition changes in ideology; a re-focusing of grievances toward class enemies, an expanded view of one's rights. . . . ■

Peter Dreier is an assistant professor of sociology at Tufts University. The above is excerpted from his article titled "Power Structures & Power Struggles" which appeared in *The Insurgent Sociologist*, Spring 1975. Copyright © by *The Insurgent Sociologist*, Dept. of Sociology, University of Oregon, Eugene, Ore. 97403. Reprinted by permission of the author.

By What Standards Do We Judge Our Struggles

From Dreier's article, and the examples he relates, it would seem that there are criteria we can use to test the adequacy of a strategy for social action. Such criteria would include the following:

1. *Does the activity benefit individuals or the working class community as a whole?*

Structural or "transitional" reforms are based not on individual victories but on collective action; achievements by groups of people working together. Structural reforms are carried out *by* a group *not on behalf* of a group. For example, consider the difference between efforts to establish a food kitchen for the destitute, as opposed to organized demands for a guaranteed annual income and the right to subsistence. The first assists individuals, but the other alters the community food system in a way which will benefit many more people. The latter also presses the demand for the basic right of people to be able to feed themselves.

2. *Does the activity simply compensate for faults within the capitalist system, or does it bring about structural reforms?*

Consider the difference between two neighborhoods. Both suffer loss of health and hygiene because of neglected trash removal. One organizes a block party to clean up the neighborhood. The people in the other neighborhood organize to demand adequate city services and sanitary living conditions. Both efforts achieve the same objective. The neighborhoods are cleaned up. But in the second neighborhood, people get a sense that they *can* "fight city hall" and change their lives through collective action. Their cynicism is decreased. Their appetite is increased for further change. They build self-confidence. Their consciousness is heightened about what they want and what the system can deliver. They see their achievement of reform as just an initial step to further organization.

3. *Does the activity serve to build class consciousness?*

Structural reforms unlike *reformist* reforms help people see their personal troubles as social problems and social problems as collective problems. Collective problems are seen as class issues, solvable in class terms. Structural reforms build class consciousness and erode legitimacy of existing authority. They challenge the official world view of those in power. They build new types of relationships among the powerless and establish a social base within the working class that can alter relations between the powerless and the powerful. Structural reforms increase people's awareness of the contradiction between human need and capital accumulation, thus, leading to greater class consciousness.

For example, adequate child care is a persistent need in working class communities. The prevailing ideology holds that this is a problem to be solved on an individual basis, or at most, within a local community. Structural change becomes possible and class consciousness becomes evident when working people begin to demand adequate care and education for all their children. Only then can mothers and fathers alike engage in productive work without having to compromise the lives of their children.

4. *Does the activity focus on the root obstacle to justice or does it mistake "the enemy"?*

Many exploited people fight each other, rather than struggle together against a common enemy. For example, in the United States, working class blacks and whites have often been set in opposition to each other to compete for jobs. Some farm workers' unions, in contrast, have seen that the basic problem they face is not the "illegal aliens" from Mexico, but rather it is the growers, the huge corporate farmers who struggle for profits rather than provide jobs and fulfill human need. The working class begins to emerge as a political force to be reckoned with when it overcomes racial and sexual divisions and all of its sectors unite.

5. *Does the activity alter the relations of power between classes?*

Structural reforms alter class relationships; the relations of production, which are at the base of the capitalist system. They also "heighten the contradictions" within capitalism, demanding things that cannot be done under capitalism without seriously undermining capital accumulation of profits. Contradictions are those strains that threaten basic institutions (class relations) and cannot be remedied by the

Written by the editors of *Christian Commitment for the '80s* for this volume.

state or any other stabilizing aspect of the social system. For example, strictly-enforced occupational health and safety laws cut down production and heighten the contradiction between the pursuit of profit and the need for decent working conditions. Similarly, full employment at prevailing union wage rates is something that capitalism cannot provide. Raising and organizing for that demand thus serves to increase our critical understanding of the incompatibility of full employment and the profit system.

The above list of strategic questions is, of course, not exhaustive. But such considerations as these must be taken into account if we are to act responsibly in the struggle for justice. Action, then critical reflection on that action, are central requirements of class-committed people. ∎

What Does a Community Do When Industry Leaves It To Die?

September 19, 1977 began as just another day in the Mahoning Valley, known around Ohio as "Steel Valley." Fifteen minutes before the day shift ended, Lykes Corporation, a New Orleans-based shipping and steel conglomerate, announced it would close its Campbell works near Youngstown. Five thousand employees would lose their jobs. The fallout would drastically cut or eliminate an additional 10,000 incomes, meaning that at least 50,000 people would be directly affected by the closing.

What happened? In this excerpt from the *JSAC Grapevine* (Vol. 9, No. 6), John Collins, a consultant to the New York-based Interfaith Center on Corporate Responsibility, describes the events leading up to the largest shutdown of a non-military plant in U.S. history.

WHAT HAPPENED?

"The Lykes Corporation acquired Youngstown Sheet & Tube in 1969. For eight years, Lykes milked Youngstown Sheet & Tube of its assets in order to acquire cash for corporate growth in other fields. In 1968, the combined debt of Youngstown Sheet & Tube and Lykes was $192 million. By 1970 it had grown to $609 million and Lykes had become a conglomerate. In the early '70s, Lykes failed to utilize available cash to modernize Youngstown, using it instead to acquire other companies — a phenomenon becoming more common as conglomerates come to dominate the national and international economy.

"When the 1973-1974 boom in steel came along, Lykes was unable to benefit fully. Its poorly maintained and unmodernized plants were unable to produce enough steel to meet customer demand, thus losing profits that could have made possible the need for modernization.

"When Lykes announced the closing in September,

it blamed cheap imports, environmental requirements and governmental price constraints. A careful review of the facts indicates that poor management practices and the draining off of profits and cash reserves for non-steel purposes were more crucial factors. Urban dwellers are familiar with landlords who buy sound buildings with borrowed money and then collect the rents for several years, refusing to provide adequate maintenance and services or to make needed repairs. When the building has fallen into disrepair, and they can't borrow on it further, the landlord walks away. When Lykes acquired it, Youngstown Sheet & Tube was a healthy company. In the ensuing eight years, Lykes' policies of heavy borrowing, siphoning off assets, mismanagement and neglect have left Youngstown Sheet & Tube an expendable part of a sick conglomerate.

"Conglomerates have no serious attachment to any particular part of their empire. They close and move plants, buy and sell companies with little regard for the consequences — except profit. But there are consequences! Steel has been made in the Mahoning Valley for over 100 years. Many steelworkers and managers are children and grandchildren of valley steelworkers. There is pride in the craft and in the tradition. Now that era is threatened, and with it the economy of the Mahoning Valley. . . .

"Statistics are impersonal, but they have consequences in human lives. The economic insecurity and loss of human dignity which ensues from the closing will be reflected in an increase in marital breakups, alcoholism, depression, racial antagonisms, crime and suicide. This is not idle speculation. Studies have demonstrated what individual-oriented therapists and caseworkers have often overlooked. There is a direct connection between 'personal' problems and economic conditions. . . ."

RELIGIOUS COMMUNITY ACTS

Youngstown might have been just another addition to the growing list of communities stricken by runaway shops, but it isn't. Youngstown is different from other communities victimized by plant closings because of the leadership taken by the religious community there in its struggle to resist.

Within a week of the closing announcement, Episcopal and Roman Catholic bishops organized a series of meetings to evaluate the situation and to formulate a response. A "Steel Crisis" conference was planned and the Ecumenical Coalition of the Mahoning Valley was formed.

Five initiatives grew which set the direction for further developments:

1. A pastoral letter was drafted which clearly stated the moral and ethical issues raised by the Lykes Corporation's decision to abandon Youngstown. The letter was to be the beginning of a local and national campaign to educate people and organize their support.

2. A study was commissioned to explore the possibility of worker/community takeover of the Campbell works, to either resume steel production or convert it to other productive purposes.

3. Advocacy of a national policy to retain basic steel and associated jobs in communities where steelworkers live was begun.

4. National attention was focused on Youngstown to develop a model for keeping jobs in other severely-affected communities.

5. The Ecumenical Coalition launched a "Save Our Valley" campaign in which everyone was encouraged to participate.

Few precedents serve as guides. The leaders of the Ecumenical Coalition are under no illusions about the challenge they face. They know they are bucking a trend that many people chalk up to unchangeable, impersonal, and irresistible economic forces. They know, however, that even economic forces are the result of decisions made by people. They have the resolve to make a difference and refuse to be content with ministering to the "personal" needs of those who suddenly find themselves unemployed.

As these words are written, the struggle at Youngstown continues. With many encouraging developments, but also with several severe setbacks, its resolution is unlikely to be conclusive. It is one episode in the widening struggle for control over the relations of production which will be waged throughout this country for much time to come.

Those who initiated the Youngstown defense planned their strategy as best they could under the pressure of crisis conditions. As one chapter in this story succeeded another they constantly tried to assess their efforts, to learn from their mistakes, to plan for a better future. How effective was the strategy developed by the Ecumenical Coalition of the Mahoning Valley?　■

The Churches and Youngstown: A Critique

by John Collins

The Youngstown project was conceived and carried out by the religious leadership of the community. While the religious community in other cities at times had responded to plant closings with apathy and despair, Youngstown gave birth to the Ecumenical Coalition of the Mahoning Valley. The Ecumenical Coalition encountered many problems; and in part because of them, its organized activity has become one of the most dramatic and significant responses to an economic crisis ever undertaken by the religious community. We can learn much from its successes and its failures.

What will the Youngstown project accomplish if it meets its goals? In answering this question it is important to note that we are applying the above criteria to two distinct phenomena: 1) the actual reopening of the mill under worker/community ownership, and 2) the Ecumenical Coalition campaign to achieve that end. The first is still possible, the second

is a reality; both are worthy of study for our purposes.

REOPENING THE MILL

Turning first to the goal of reopening the mill, let us note precisely what is intended. First, a mill destined for the scrap heap by its previous owners would be purchased at a fraction of what a new mill would cost. Within a few months, after only minor repairs, 1,600 workers could reopen the mill and produce one million tons of steel products per year from steel slabs.

After installation of an electric furnace in the second year, the mill could compete with more advanced facilities. It would then make its own steel from scrap and also employ an additional 1,000 workers.

Financing the entire effort would require about $30 million in private investment, $27 million in direct grants from state and Federal government, and federally-guaranteed loans of over $200 million. Ownership of the new company, Community Steel, Inc., would be shared by investors, workers and the Youngstown community. It would be controlled by a board of 15 directors. Private investors would elect six representatives, labor would elect another six and a locally-controlled community development corporation would name the final three.

John Collins is a lawyer and Methodist clergyperson who has worked for the Interfaith Center on Corporate Responsibility. He is presently serving as Co-Director of Clergy and Laity Concerned. The above article was commissioned by the editors for this volume. At the time of its writing, May 1979, the Carter administration had already turned down the request for the loan guarantees needed to purchase the Campbell work mill and reopen it under worker/community ownership. Efforts continue to reverse the decision and implement the project.

Development of a fully-integrated, worker/community owned steel mill would have profound and far-reaching effects. Placing worker representatives on the board of directors could begin to change the basic nature of property relations between owners and workers and make possible a workplace which does not exploit workers. While the plan, in part, calls for worker *ownership*, the issue of worker participation in *management and control at the shop floor level* is clearly an issue which must be addressed as the project develops.

These changed relations would make possible a new worker consciousness stemming from the discovery that they can operate a steel mill efficiently, just as the General Motors sit-down strikers of the 1930s found that they could run the auto plants without the bosses. Much of the power of U.S. capitalism rests on the carefully cultivated myth that the economy will fall apart without capitalist management. Fear that this myth would be shattered is a significant motivation behind Big Steel's opposition to the Youngstown plan. Community Steel would also serve as a measure for judging the performance and pricing of other steel companies, just as public power companies have provided a way of evaluating private utilities.

Finally, if the mill is successful, that is, if it can pay wages and debts and keep operating, it would be a powerful model for other communities with similar problems. Tens of thousands of jobs have been lost since World War II because corporations simply locked their gates and moved away. It is not difficult to imagine steelworkers holding training sessions in Youngstown and traveling to other cities to agitate for worker/community control. In these ways the mill would build class consciousness, focus on basic obstacles to justice and move clearly toward a better economic system than that prevailing today.

CRITICISM LEFT AND RIGHT

Despite these strong arguments in its favor, the Youngstown project has been frequently criticized — most often from the Right, as can be expected — but also from the Left. The criticisms are of two kinds: 1) whether the project can work as planned and 2) whether it is sufficiently radical to deal with the basic problems of capitalism. Marxists have made the second criticism, maintaining that the only viable solution is nationalization of the entire steel industry. They say the plan only compensates for faults within the system, rather than moving toward a better one. This criticism raises the issue between state ownership and control, on the one hand, and local decentralized ownership and control by workers and communities on the other.

The Youngstown project appeals not only to those who oppose big business, but also to those who

complain about big government. Despite the concept of local control, the plan calls for the Federal government to provide the essential loan guarantees. The failure to fully face this contradiction has been a serious one and may yet be a major cause of the project's failure. To achieve structural reform in either housing, education or jobs, major outlays of capital are required. The Federal government is a major source of such outlays, but it is controlled by powerful corporate interests. Oil and gas deregula-

tion, the expanding military budget, in addition to the defeat of labor law reform and a consumer protection agency are but a few recent examples indicating who really runs the country.

Another criticism of the project is that it is not feasible: The plant is too old; Big Steel will not permit it to compete; steel is a sick industry; the workers are being asked to pay for the neglect of the previous owners; etc. These are all serious criticisms, but they are factual rather than tactical. In evaluating any proposed strategy, it is important to ask *what will work?* What can be said for the Ecumenical Coalition on this point is that they asked for and got sufficient advice from steel industry technicians, former management personnel and noted economists. The weight of the evidence is so strongly in favor of the plan that it should be given a chance to prove itself. The Ecumenical Coalition deserves credit for making a commitment and taking calculated risks in an area where church leaders usually avoid involvement.

PROBLEMS ENCOUNTERED

An evaluation of the actual campaign mounted by the Ecumenical Coalition, in light of our criteria, is helpful in understanding many of the problems faced.

First, the Ecumenical Coalition is a loose association of clergy from the Youngstown area. Uniting so quickly around such a crisis was so unprecedented that it tended to obscure the deep ideological divisions among many members and the lack of any economic analysis on the part of others. From the beginning, there was no clear consensus on the fundamental purpose and long-term goals of the coalition. For some, the sole priority was to restore jobs to the laid-off workers. Whether the mill was purchased by private Japanese interests or through a worker/community ownership plan mattered little. Others saw the closing as symptomatic of a deep crisis in the general economy. They supported the plan as a means to develop alternatives to the present system of absentee corporate ownership. Still others saw the proposal as one step in the struggle for socialism.

Most of the time, these differences were papered over, but they had some serious effects. For example, there were various proposals for education and organizing among the churches and within the Youngstown community. Most of these programs never came to be, partly because internal agreement could not be reached on the question of the educational content and the rationale for organizing. Despite normally heavy workloads and the pressure of additional commitments, coalition members should have taken time to resolve their internal differences. The Ecumenical Coalition lost an opportunity to build class consciousness, and with it, an important grass roots base in the Youngstown community.

A related problem was the Ecumenical Coalition's failure to include steelworkers until very late in the process. The plan was devised *on behalf of*, rather than *by* working class people. The clerical coalition was ambivalent and showed the classic reluctance of religious leaders to take clear sides in labor struggles. Had the Ecumenical Coalition sought to organize the unemployed steelworkers from the beginning, rather than 15 months after the plant closing, there would be different results today.

When struggling for structural reform, it is essential to achieve unity in clearly identifying the enemy. In Youngstown, some of the Protestant coalition members had business leaders in their congregations, and so they tried to walk a tightrope between supporting the Ecumenical Coalition and offending their church membership. They took pains to avoid

socialist language and ideology, even to the point of calling the plan "Plymouth Rock Capitalism." Therefore, while most of the leading clergy at times shared the vision that they might be able, in the words of one, "to turn this country around," they were prevented from being guided by that vision by disagreement in the coalition as to the real enemy — not just Lykes or Big Steel, but the present system of corporate capitalism.

Despite these problems, the Ecumenical Coalition's campaign has been notable in several respects. Its early Pastoral Letter was an indictment of the corporate system which makes tragedies like Youngstown inevitable. It was a powerful moral indictment of *corporate*, not individual, behavior strongly measured against the yardstick of the ethical teachings of the Bible.

The Youngstown project met the test of two of our criteria very well. Initially, by daring to put forth the plan for a worker-owned mill, it raised a new consciousness among its participants as to what might be possible. As we have studied, one of the initial obstacles the coalition faced was the difficulty its members and many of the workers had in even imagining that they could buy and successfully operate a steel mill — but they refused to be discouraged.

Secondly, throughout the campaign, the Ecumenical Coalition focused on a basic obstacle to justice: The unacceptability and immorality of the corporate shutdown. It met Lyke's insistence that it had no other choice with a plan of its own designed to show that the mill could operate and could do successfully without capitalist bosses. In this sense, the Ecumenical Coalition of the Mahoning Valley marks a significant departure from so many church responses to economic problems — usually the band-aid variety.

Two other smaller factories in Youngstown have been taken over by workers in the past 18 months. Both were strongly influenced by the pacesetting work and goals of the Ecumenial Coalition of the Mahoning Valley. Other consequences will follow.

■

Group Exercise

This final session of *Must We Choose Sides?* provides an opportunity to critically evaluate the activity of your own group. Select two or more struggles for social reform in which members of the group are involved. The more familiarity most of the group has with these activities, the more productive the discussion.

It is necessary to evaluate the political impact of reforms. Using the five criteria given, make an assessment of strategy and tactics. Are your efforts for progressive social change circumscribed within the limits of the capitalist system, only defined in terms of *what can be*? Or are they conceived in view of *what should be* in terms of human needs and demands? How can struggles for *reformist* reforms be transformed into class conscious *structural* reforms?

Can your group suggest better objectives and methods of struggle to advance the cause of social justice? Bear in mind that people involved in any program may have a vested interest in the way they are doing things, and can be expected to be somewhat defensive about the intent and consequences of their activity. Criticism and self-criticism are both essential.

You have now completed the six self-guided sessions of this study volume. It is a rather unique contribution to the field of Christian social mission. Undoubtedly your group has some strong opinions about its strengths and weaknesses. The editors would appreciate your comments and criticism. Please draft an evaluation letter, including background information about your group, and send it to:

> The Interreligious Task Force For Social Analysis
> P.O. Box 359
> Ambler, PA 19002   Thank you.

Looking critically at our world, considering how it might be more humane and taking the necessary steps to change it are most responsible activities. They are the lifelong tasks of a committed people. In the Appendix that follows you will find a wealth of suggestions for continuing study, for continuing analysis, for continuing involvement. The editors of this guide have also prepared a sequel entitled, *Christian Commitment for the '80s: Which Side Are We On?* It has been designed to advance the discussion begun in this volume. We encourage you to continue. See page 127 for an order form.

Appendix

The following are offered as a partial listing of sources for further study or involvement. It is by no means a complete list of what is available in publications, films, or organizations.

BIBLIOGRAPHY

SESSION 1

Let Me Speak: Testimony of a Woman of the Bolivian Mines, Domitila Barrios de Chungara, Monthly Review Press, 1978.

All the Livelong Day, Barbara Garson, Penguin Books, New York, 1977.

Pink Collar Workers, Louise Kapp Howe, Putnam Books, New York, 1977.

Working: People Talk About What They Do All Day and How They Feel About What They Do, Studs Terkel, Avon Books, 1975.

SESSION 2

False Promises: The Shaping of American Working Class Consciousness, Stanley Aronowitz, McGraw-Hill, 1973.

Global Reach: The Power of the Multi-national Corporations, Richard J. Barnet & Ronald E. Muller, Simon & Schuster, 1974

Labor and Monopoly Capital: The Degradation of Work in the Twentieth Century, Harry Braverman, Monthly Review Press, 1974.

Who Rules America?, G. William Domhoff, Prentice-Hall, 1967. (Especially Chapter 1, "The American Upper Class.")

The Hidden Injuries of Class, Richard Sennett & Jonathan Cobb, Vintage Books, Random House, 1972.

SESSIONS 3 AND 4

Christians and Marxists, Jose Miguez Bonino, William B. Eerdmans Press, 1976.

Understanding Marxism, Frank Cunningham, Progress Books, Toronto, 1978.

Doing Theology in a New Key, Robert McAfee Brown, Westminster, 1978.

The Capitalist System, Richard C. Edwards, Michael Reich, Thomas E. Weisskopf, editors, Prentice-Hall, 1978.

Frontiers of Theology in Latin America, R. Gibellini, editor, Orbis Books, 1979.

The Enemy, Felix Greene, Random House, 1970.

The Rich and the Super-Rich, Ferdinand Lundberg, Bantam Books, 1968.

Poor People's Movements: Why They Succeed, How They Fail, Frances Fox Piven & Richard A. Cloward, Vintage Books, 1979.

The Corporate Captivity of the Church, Zacchaeus Collective, c/o Collective, 4527 N. Malden, Chicago, IL, 1976.

SESSION 5

Doing Theology in a Revolutionary Situation, Jose Miguez Bonino, Fortress Press, 1975.

Theology in the Americas, John Eagleson & Sergio Torres, editors, Orbis Books, 1976.

The Radical Kingdom, Rosemary Ruether. Paulist, 1975.

Marx and the Bible, Jose Miranda, Orbis Books, 1975.

Manual: *Is Liberation Theology for North America?: The Response of First World Churches,* Theology in the Americas, 1978.

Theology of a Nomad Church, Hugo Assmann, Orbis Books, 1976.

Black Church in the Americas, Hart Nelsen, editor, Basic Books, 1971.

You Can Be Set Free, Roy Sano, United Methodist Publishing House, 1977.

SESSION 6

Getting Into the Act, Frederick Wentz, Abington Press, 1978.

To Hear and To Heed, Urban Bishops Coalition, Detroit, 1978.

ADDITIONAL BOOKS OF INTEREST

U.S. Capitalism in Crisis, Economic Education Project of the Union of Radical Political Economists (URPE), New York, 1978.

Marxism and the Metropolis: New Perspectives in Urban Political Economy, William K. Tabb & Larry Sawyers, editors, Oxford University Press, New York, 1978.

Women's Work Is . . ., Bobbi Wells Hargleroad & Linda A. Hall, editors, Institute on Church in Urban-Industrial Mission, Chicago, IL, 1978.

Imperialism from the Colonial Age to the Present, Harry Magdoff, Monthly Review Press, New York, 1978.

How Capitalism Works, Pierre Jalee, Monthly Review Press, 1977.

Economics: Mainstream Reading & Radical Critiques, David Mermelstein, editor, Random House, New York, 1976.

The Economics Crisis Reader: Understanding Depression, Inflation, Unemployment, Energy, Food, Wage & Price Controls and Other Disorders of World Capitalism, David Mermelstein, editor, Vintage Books, 1975.

The Working Class Majority, Andrew Levisson, Penguin, 1975.

Christian Political Theology: A Marxian Guide, Joseph Petulla, Orbis Books, Maryknoll, NY, 1972.

The World of the Blue Collar Worker, Irving Howe, editor, New York Times Quadrangle Books, 1972.

Labor's Untold Story, Richard O. Boyer & Herbert M. Morais, United Electrical, Radio & Machine Workers of America, New York, 1971.

Political Economy, John Eaton, International Publishers, New York, 1973.

The Essential Works of Marxism, Bantam Books, 1961.

PERIODICALS

Christianity and Crisis, a monthly journal of liberal opinion, 537 W. 121st St., New York, NY 10027. $12/year.

Sojourners, a monthly evangelical journal concerned with the Christian witness in society. 1029 Vermont Ave. N.W., Washington, DC 20005. $12/year.

JSAC Grapevine, a monthly bulletin (except August and December) published by the Joint Strategy & Action Committee, Inc. This committee is a coalition of national mission agencies of the major Protestant denominations. Each bulletin focuses on a particular issue in the society and connects the issue to the Church's mission. 475 Riverside Dr. Room 1700A, New York, NY 10027.

NACLA Report on the Americas, a bi-monthly magazine of in-depth studies, well-researched and documented, clearly written and powerfully illustrated. Each issue focuses on a major issue or country in the Americas, primarily in Latin America. 151 W. 19th St., 9th floor, New York, NY 10011. $11/year.

Social Questions Bulletin, a bi-monthly bulletin published since 1911, which reports on crucial social and denominational issues for the Methodist Federation for Social Action. 76 Clinton Ave., Staten Island, NY 10301. $5/year.

THE WITNESS magazine, is an independent, ecumenical advocacy journal for social issues. It is published monthly by the Episcopal Church Publishing Company, P.O. Box 359, Ambler, PA 19002. $9/year.

Radical Religion, a quarterly publication serving the progressive religious community and committed to the global development of liberation theology and the international movement for socialism. P.O. Box 9164, Berkeley, CA 94709. $9/year.

Justice Ministries: Resources for Urban Mission, published by the Institute of the Church in Urban Industrial Society, 5700 S. Woodlawn Ave., Chicago, IL 60637. $8/year.

FILMS

Controlling Interest. A 45-minute, 16 mm. film, subject of which is described in its subtitle: *The World of the Multi-national Corporations* (MNCs). It shows the impact of MNCs in the lives of working people in Latin America and the U.S. Included are interviews with MNC representatives, plus the effect of MNCs in Brazil, Chile, and the Dominican Republic. Accompanied by a Study Guide. Rental fee, $30-$55, or can be negotiated. Order through California Newsreel, 630 Natoma St., San Francisco, CA 94103.

Guess Who's Coming for Breakfast. Film strip, cassette. Available from the Interfaith Center for Corporate Responsibility, 475 Riverside Drive, New York, NY 10027. Using the Dominican Republic as a case study, it raises the question, "What is the role of the multi-national corporation in supporting economic injustices abroad to keep prices high for U.S.-based investors?"

Crystal Lee Jordan. A 20-minute, 16 mm color film describing the life of Crystal Lee Jordan, a key figure who helped to organize J. P. Stevens workers in the South. Crystal Lee Jordan was the union organizer upon whose life the film *Norma Rae* was supposedly based. See the real person in this film. $10 rental fee. Available from Indiana University Audio-Visual Center, Bloomington, IN 47401.

Come a Long Way to Stand Here. One-hour film strip, cassette with study guide for theological reflection and economic analysis. Available from Theology in the Americas, 475 Riverside Drive, Room 1268, New York, NY 10027. A series of four interviews with a black, Hispanic, white and Panamanian working woman. Rental fee $30; purchase price $60.

Sharing Global Resources. Available as a 40 minute film strip or slide show. (Slide show also available in Spanish.) *Sharing Global Resources* examines the confrontation between developing countries and multi-national corporations, focusing on two case studies: Chile and Jamaica and the role of MNCs in each. It asks audiences hard questions such as how can U.S. citizens be responsive and responsible to global demands for a more equitable sharing of resources and to similar demands from the poor at home? Can humanity find a peaceful way to share the earth's resources? Purchase price, $50 for slide shows, $45 for film strip. One week rentals available for either form at $10. Rentals and purchases accompanied by a study action guide and documentation. Order from NARMIC, 1501 Cherry St., Philadelphia, PA 19102.

GAMES

Class Struggle, a game by Bertell Ollman, available from Class Struggle, Inc., 487 Broadway, New York, NY 10013. An interesting break from monopoly.

Starpower. Simulation game for illustrating the dynamics of power/powerlessness, reform/revolution; competitive/cooperative economic institutions, etc. Available from Simile II, P.O. Box 1023, La Jolla, CA 92037.

ORGANIZATIONS

American Friends Service Committee (AFSC), the Quaker organization for social action and mission work which has been active for many years in movements of peace and justice. For information about the various projects of AFSC write to 1501 Cherry St., Philadelphia, PA 19102. (215) 241-7000.

Catholic Committee on Urban Ministry, a network of Catholic priests, religious and laity bound by the commitment to work for justice within church and society. It provides workshops and training sessions at the local level on urban affairs; resource to diocesan urban affairs offices on urban questions and problems; communication through bulletins and reports on current issues. It promotes the formation of regional networks of social ministers as sources of support, mutual assistance, analysis and reflection. 1112 Memorial Library, University of Notre Dame, Notre Dame, IN 46556. (219) 283-3293.

Christians For Socialism (formerly American Christians Toward Socialism—ACTS). CFS was formed in the U.S. in 1974 as part of the international movement of CFS. Its locally-based chapters provide for regular theoretical study, praxis reflection and celebration of faith within their groups. CFS is a movement, not a party or a church, committed to a class option in support of the interests of the poor and working people of the U.S. CFS is committed to liberate the churches from the economic and cultural bonds of capitalism and to building socialism rooted in the U.S. democratic traditions. For further information on the movement of CFS or for chapter-forming information and papers from the U.S. groups, call or write CFS National Office, 3540 14th St., Detroit, MI 48208. (313) 833-3987.

Church & Society Network, an informal association of Episcopalians and others working at the social mission of the church. For more information about group formation and program, write P.O. Box 359, Ambler, PA 19002. (215) 643-7067.

Coalition for a New Foreign and Military Policy, is a network of citizens, national and religious organizations working to promote arms control and disarmament, reduce military spending and protect human rights. It coordinates the work of multiple groups at critical moments in order to influence legislation in Congress and the Administration. It sends packets of information to contact groups and individuals on legislative developments and upcoming issues. 120 Maryland Ave. N.E., Washington, DC 20002. (202) 546-8400.

Interfaith Center for Corporate Responsibility, monitors the social effects of corporations' policies and works to influence corporate policy through dialogue and stockholder resolutions. 475 Riverside Dr., New York, NY 10027.

Lutheran New Wine Exchange, is an informational network for "edge of the church" Lutherans involved in justice work in the U.S. with the primary goal of building international consciousness and political-economic analysis in order to question the effect of these two things on domestic justice. It publishes a newsletter and conducts two theology conferences a year. 437 E. 140th St., New York, NY 10454. (212) 585-6084.

Methodist Federation For Social Action, is an independent movement working within the United Methodist Church since 1907 to promote social action in the church and work for a society not based on the struggle for profit. The Federation has eight area chapters and publishes the bi-monthly *Social Questions Bulletin.* It is giving special attention to combatting politically reactionary tendencies in the denomination. 76 Clinton Ave., Staten Island, NY 10301 (212) 273-4941.

National Convergence of Justice and Peace Centers, is a predominantly Catholic network of centers, offices, commissions and organizations joined together for communication and joint action. The Convergence includes groups with a national constituency, some oriented to specific constituencies or locales, as well as some diocesan offices of Justice & Peace. Member groups share in special projects proposed by participating groups; on-going legislative efforts; clearing house for organizations and committees desiring contacts in the initial period of establishing justice and peace efforts.

Theology in the Americas is a five-year ecumenical program for the contextualization of theology in the Americas. Books, documents, film strips, newsletters and models for theological reflection are available from the nine projects working toward a synthesis to overcome racism, sexism, classism and imperialism. The nine projects are: The Black Theology Project; The Hispanic Theology Project; Women, Work and the Economy; The Asian-American Project; The Native American Project; Theologians Task Force; Church and Labor Dialogue; Alternative Theology Project; Ecumenical Dialogue of Third World Theologians. For more information: 475 Riverside Dr., Room 1268, New York, NY 10027. (212) 870-2078.

World Student Christian Federation is a world-wide coalition of student Christian movements committed to progressive political activity as motivated by a radical faith perspective. The *North American Region* publishes a quarterly newspaper, *Press On!*, and works through programs and projects of movements throughout Canada and the U.S. WSCF encourages participation of all students who are interested in issues of education, students and labor, and international solidarity. Write WSCF-NA, 427 Bloor St. W., Toronto, Ontario, Canada M5S 1X7. (416) 922-8597 or (415) 548-8312.

RESEARCH AND INFORMATION CENTERS

Investigative Resource Center, is a tax-exempt organization founded to meet the information needs of labor and community activists, organizers and researchers engaged in educating and mobilizing constituencies around vital public policy issues. It has two major projects: *The Data Center* is an independent, non-profit library focusing on the global political economy. The Data Center collection is organized to reflect the struggle between capital and labor. It provides information services on major corporations, banks, industries, and the struggle to resist these dominant forces of capitalism by labor and liberation movements. The staff will conduct file searches on the subject of your inquiry and send photo copies by mail. Fees vary according to the amount of time spent and the ability to pay. *Information Services on Latin America* (ISLA) has been a valuable resource for 9 years for anyone who needs to know about socio-economic and political developments in Latin America. ISLA provides monthly mailings of articles on Latin America from nine major newspapers of the English language press. Write for subscription rates. Investigative Resource Center, 464 19th Street, Oakland, CA 94612. Data Center (415) 835-4692. ISLA (415) 835-0678.

New York CIRCUS is a specialized ministry based in New York City, working within the progressive Latin American community. It develops, primarily through the work of exiles, a packet of materials and translations of articles designed to build solidarity between Christians struggling for liberation. N.Y. CIRCUS also conducts seminars on liberation theology. P.O. Box 37, Times Square Station, New York, NY 10036. Phone (212) 663-5012.